TONY SHERIDAN

The one The Beatles called

'The Teacher'

Nobody planned it.
That's the way the 60's were.

Colin Crawley

Acknowledgements and thanks:

I wish to thank all those who have helped in many ways with what was not an easy book to put together, including Tony Sheridans family: Tony Sheridan junior in America, Kathy Hussein in Norfolk, England and Rosie Sheridan Mac Ginnity in Hamburg, Germany. Also many thanks to Horst Fascher in Hamburg for his help and guidance during those early band years.

I would like to thank Ulf Kruger for much of his useful information and assistance. Hans Olof Gottfridsson in Sweden for his invaluable help.Kuno Dreysse for his important radio programmes and interviews. And of course old friends Fritz Schoeder (the only German I have ever met named Fritz!) and Kalli Calinski for much their unselfish help during those early years.

I also owe so much to Ingrid, my dear German wife, who suffered silently during my years of writing and put up with my many frustrations and moods. Most of all I would like to thank my son Christian and his clever partner Kirsty van Lieshout for answering my questions about how to press the right buttons on the computer and more importantly preparing this book for publication.

To all those many people who helped Tony Sheridan and his bands over the years and whose names I no longer recall (due to age and hard living!) I extend a big thank you!

Kind regards,

Colin Crawley

TONY SHERIDAN
Personal-Manager HORST FASCHER
STAR-CLUB · HAMBURG · GROSSE FREIHEIT 39

PROLOGUE

Every now and again: or possibly only once in a person's lifetime, we stumble across a talent so rare, so completely unusual, so out of the ordinary, and so very different, that we are unable to forget them. You may not like the person behind the talent at all, but even so there is something about them that draws you to them, and allows you to overcome your dislike or prejudice against them. It is strange that we can love a person without liking them and like a person without loving them. Tony Sheridan was one of those special people who was able to fascinate and hold an audience spellbound: which is what happened to me on seeing him for the first time at the '2 i's' coffee bar in London. Afterwards I would never be the same again. It is hard to explain what had happened, except to say I was hooked and wanted to watch him play, sing and perform again and again. But to those on the receiving end of his unpredictable behaviour – Tony was just a dangerous driver looking for a car crash. Later he told me himself he really was a 'loose cannon', and I could see he was sincere about what he was saying, which puzzled me until I knew him better.

It is one of the mysteries of human nature that we sometimes see only what we want to see: good or bad. But we all have the right to make up our own minds about everything and anyone. My opinion may not be the same as your own, and yours may not be the same as mine. But who cares? We tell it as we see it; which is the honest and the only way. You may think, after reading what I have to say about Tony Sheridan and his connection with the Beatles, that with friends like me, who needs enemies? But my story would be incomplete if I didn't tell you about the different sides to Tony's character, painful as it may be to those who cared so much for him as I did. It is better to hear an account given by a well-meaning friend than the ramblings of a hostile enemy, but I promise to stick only to what I know. I knew Tony very well and he knew me; we were friends from the start , since he and I joined the 'Jets' – the first British rock 'n roll band to visit Germany.

I have been angry with him only once in the four wild, fantastic, life-changing years we played together, and it led to a fight. There were other unforeseen interruptions during that time, like when we were thrown out or asked to leave the places we played at, which meant finding work elsewhere. We began our rock and roll careers in the London cellar clubs: he in the famous 2'i's and I in the nearby Top Ten club where the 'Jets, were formed.

1. SOHO

The 60's as we know were momentous times in the history of popular music. Tony Sheridan and I were there at the beginning and he became a huge part of my life. Even after I had got married and returned to England, we still kept in touch: exchanging letters and passing on information about what we were doing. To some of these letters I shall refer later. Sadly there was a darker side to Tony too, which contradicted everything I knew about him. I will tell you about that, too, or my story will be incomplete.

But first let me go back to where it all started, when I first saw Tony Sheridan play in the London district of Soho. I was home on leave from the Merchant Navy and heard about a great rock 'n' roll club called the "2'i's" and rushed there to see if it was really as good as people were saying. It was once a meeting place for the trendy 'coffee bar' set, but times had moved on and the coffee bars had become 'old school' and no longer in fashion.

The owners needed to try something new and brought in live 'skiffle' bands, playing Lonnie Donegan's music: Tony loved this! 'Nobody's child', sung by Lonnie, was one of Tony's all time favourite songs. I found out later it had real meaning for him in his own life, and this was why he always sang it with great emotion. But for the young it was rock 'n' roll they now preferred above all else, and it was here to stay.

The owners of the cellar clubs in London wasted no time bringing in the new music as an alternative to the tame, shallow imitations of 'rock' played by dance bands in the glitzy Locarno, or Mecca ballrooms, where many of the young would meet – having nowhere else to go. The cellar clubs of Soho became the places the young wanted to be. It was where the 'real' music was being played. The music we had loved from the very beginning.

Tony Sheridan was on stage when I first walked in. I squeezed my way through the crowd in a haze of cigarette smoke and noisy amplifiers, to get as near as possible to the stage.

I watched fascinated as Tony, aged 19, strutted his stuff: full of confidence, ability and flair. He owned the stage; what struck me even more was the intensity of emotion in his voice, and his exciting and expressive guitar playing. It was also his ability to accompany himself as he sang, not only while playing the rhythm riffs, but the lead guitar parts as well. Not once did I see him look down at his guitar while playing: it was something I had never witnessed anyone else do before.

Added to this was his riveting presence.

I looked around and saw no one was able to take their eyes off him. He seemed to exude a strange magnetic force: an overpowering attraction. Elvis had heaps of the same thing, but for me and for those watching, Tony Sheridan had it too.

Obviously his talent was different from Elvis, but he had the same indefinable something, which is present in all truly talented artists. Without this special something, all other artists are put in the shade: relegating them to the 'quite good', or the 'ordinary'.

Staying all evening, I listened intently as he sang one song after another with great feeling. I watched everything he did: trying to analyse exactly what he was doing to me, and those around me, making us feel this way. I couldn't get enough of him, and stayed to the end of his session: when someone else took over, someone who was nowhere near so good.

No other singer or guitarist that came after him that evening could compare with the inimitable Tony Sheridan and I was hooked – becoming a regular at the 2 'i's: and always looking out for him. During this time I was just a spectator, coming and going on different ships to and from the port of London – I was then in the Merchant Navy.

Much of the time Tony wasn't there, and no one knew where he was. Others told me he had been in constant demand: working with The Shadows, Cliff Richard and others. Helping with studio work or he was on UK tours with various American artists.

These tiny insignificant and scruffy London cellar clubs had, from nothing, become schools of modern music for the up-and-coming British singers and musicians of the day. Among them were many of the most successful, including The Beatles. The two main clubs were the 2'i's or the 'Top Ten': where most performed without pay: they did it because they loved it – which is the best reason for doing anything creative. They included Rick Hardy, The Vipers, Marty Wilde, Vince Taylor, Terry Dene, Vince Eager, Billy Fury and Adam Faith.

Tony Sheridan played alongside most of them at various times, and many of them went on to appear on the BBC TV rock 'n' roll shows produced by Jack Good including: 'Oh Boy', 'Boy meets Girls,' and 'Six – Five Special'.

The influential Jack Good was also the manager of many of the artists who appeared on his shows, and they would become world stars. If Jack liked you, you were 'in'. He saw Tony's talent at the 2'i's soon after Tony arrived in London from Norfolk, and invited him to appear in one of his BBC 'live' shows ('Oh Boy'). Tony became a regular there. The BBC should have been Tony's launching pad to stardom, which Tony, because of his talent, justly deserved. But it didn't turn out that way.

The unforgivable happened and Tony messed up. Proving to be unreliable and difficult to handle – famously turning up late for a Jack Good show without his guitar, only minutes before he was due to appear on a 'live' television show, where timing was of the essence.

'Lend me your guitar man, I'm on in a minute', he pleaded with the other bands.

This was too much for Jack the producer and Tony, despite his talent, was dropped from the show.

It was to be the start of a long sequence of missed opportunities, but this was the first big one, and Tony was to ruin other chances of world fame. There was no question about whether or not he deserved the opportunities he created. His talent cried out for recognition, but his behaviour always got in the way. Tony Sheridan became a mystery to everyone. Many others less talented artists were passing him by and leaving him behind.

But every time I heard him play I was transfixed; his shows made such a great impact, not just on me, but on everyone: compelling them to go back to see him once more. On stage he seemed to be in another world: intense, emotional, penetrating and wild. He meant every word he sang, and I felt every note he played.

From then on, Soho is where you would find me, whenever I was home from the sea. After saying hello to my family, I would race to be first in the 2'i's audience, standing as close to the stage as possible: watching and waiting for Tony to arrive, but more often he didn't come and I felt alone. There were always other good musicians waiting in the wings for a chance to replace those on stage, but none as good as Tony Sheridan.

In those early days there was never a shortage of talent – just a constant procession of new rock 'n' rollers queuing to get up on stage to show what they can do – hoping someone was in the audience watching and waiting for someone new with something different, who they could make into a star.

One singer or guitarist would leave the stage and another take his place. There were few complete bands in those days, mostly lone musicians, and they all wanted to play or sing on stage so as to be noticed. Some were paid (a miserly ten shillings a night), but most got nothing at all. But it wasn't about the money, they just wanted to play or sing. The music had taken over their lives.

Excitement always grew whenever Tony Sheridan climbed up onto the stage. I noticed how he always ignored his audience. They forgave him for that, and in return he gave them a great show, leaving everyone clamouring for more.

Tony was the most unlikeliest rock 'n' roller; his life in Norfolk was a complete contrast to that of a rock star. As a boy he was a member of the church choir, a violin player, leader of the sixth form school orchestra, which was deeply into classical music, as well as the madrigal group (an ancient form of unaccompanied song). He was also involved in the school's Gilbert & Sullivan productions and also was a member of both the Scouts and the British Red Cross. He was a good Grammar School boy and did all that was expected of him; except he turned out to be a disappointment to his mother, who hoped for better things.

Rock music for Tony may have began as a reaction to his mothers hopes of a career for him in classical music. It was she who paid for his first violin lessons in the quiet of the
Cathedral Close in Norwich: a city where he and his family lived an orderly life – as did most young grammar school boys before him, in the days before rock 'n' roll came along.

Tony upset the carefully made plans of a career in music his mother had made for her son; Tony was not going to become a Yehudi Menuhin just to please her. He was clearly no ordinary boy. There was a fire within him that couldn't be put out. An unquenchable urge to break free and plunge into a more exciting life on the wild side of rock 'n roll. That's how it started for most of us, to varying degrees. I myself was never wild, my parents didn't allow me to be: but I did feel something tremendous was happening to me and many others.

Tony just wanted to have fun, to experience new things, to get together with the youth of the day, in the same way as youth did the world over in the 1960's. Now we had our own music, which most of our parents hated – We were glad they did. There was revolution in the air! And all at once the views of our parents didn't matter any more.

It wasn't long before Tony found his way to the 2'i's cellar club in Soho, and became part of the music scene there. He, too, was paid the ten shillings a night in those early days of the cellar clubs, but was soon to be earning a lot more.

I was there at the 2'i's when Tony climbed up onto the tiny stage to entertain a large audience made up mainly of students. They had all heard about this new boy and were unusually hushed: as if they knew what was coming. Tony exuded the look of someone brimming with confidence and authority, someone who knew what he was doing.

He slowly began tuning his guitar, in no rush whatsoever, as the excited and expectant crowd looked on. Standing still at first, he looked around him then nodded to the on-stage musicians before unleashing an explosion of sound, with the song 'Whole Lotta Shakin'.

The club atmosphere was charged with electricity. The audience was stunned; my hair felt as though it was standing on end and my body tingled all over. I stood there paralysed and open-mouthed, absolutely blown away by this raw and effortlessly music, as Tony raced from one standard classic rock 'n' roll number to another. His legs shook and wobbled, his face was pained and contorted. Unable to tear myself away I was forced to stay where I was until the very end, not leaving until the club closed, and still mesmerized by this obvious star-to-be, whose name most of those present that evening didn't know.

At the end of the evening I walked across Tower Bridge to my home in Bermondsey in a happy trance; Tony Sheridan's music still thumping in my head. I knew I must see him again when I was next home from the sea. But for a long time afterwards, as my ship sailed for the Amazon, I couldn't get him out of my mind. I began spending more of my free time on the ship's upper decks; wrestling with a cheap Spanish guitar I had bought in Las Palmas.

I was determined to learn new chords to add to the ones I already knew, and joined the young deck-hands who, like me, had the same interest in learning to play the guitar as I did. They too had been hooked on the new music, and couldn't get enough of it.

But practising at sea was frustrating and difficult. Hardly anyone knew more than three chords, and unlike the 'landlubbers' we couldn't find anyone to teach us. But once back in London; I quickly said hello to my family before rushing off as soon as I could to the 2'i's.

But as had happened too many times already, Tony Sheridan wasn't there, and no one knew where he was – and of course, I was devastated.

While at the 2 'i's I saw a young Cliff Richard on stage imitating Elvis; Cliff had long sideburns then, as well as a fixed sneer, trying to look mean and aggressive. It wasn't working. Around his neck hung a huge gold chain. Cliff played his own guitar in those early days and sang very well, even though it was a little tame for some of us. Cliff was never a hard-core rocker, but I could see he was very popular, and always had a large noisy fan club in the audience. He did make a great rock number, 'Move it', which most of the early rock-bands played, and which would make Cliff long remembered together with other great songs he recorded over the years.

Still looking out for Tony, I watched as a fresh band of young talent were vying with each other to get onto the stage star into the limelight – all hoping to be spotted by someone important, who could make them a star.

There was no sign of Tony Sheridan and I was beginning to give up hope of ever seeing him again. Eventually I did get tired of looking for him and found another cellar club called the 'Top Ten', where there was a very good 'regular' band. The club was in Berwick Street and from there I could quickly go back to the 2 'i's, should Tony Sheridan suddenly appear there again.

However I did to return one last time to the 2'i's hoping to get some more information on Tony's whereabouts and was told, by someone who knew him well, that Tony was definitely on tour with Gene Vincent and Eddie Cochran. I went back to sea again and continued practising on board with my Spanish guitar, learning as much as I could.

It was like a ritual – whenever I was back in Soho I couldn't resist looking for Tony in every club and café I could find and also any other places where rock musicians might hang out. Hoping that just by chance, I would accidentally bump into him. The rest of my evenings were spent at the 'Top Ten' club, and then it was back to sea again.

But something unbelievable and very special happened to me the next time I was home from the sea. Even when I think about it now, it still seems absolutely incredible as to how it came about, and how much it would completely change my life and lead to me playing alongside a great star. That fairy tale evening began when I again ended up at the 'Top Ten' where the 'regular' band was playing.

On that special evening the club was unusually busy and once inside I was hit by a blast of hot air caused by the small, grossly overcrowded room, filled with hot sweaty students. There was standing room only: as it was in a small area not designed to accommodate so many people. But everyone was having a great time; I was in a place where I wanted to be – close to the stage, and straight away feeling completely at home and at ease.

In the main room was a stage where a band was playing – much too loudly, but it didn't matter: I liked it like that. It was no different from the 2 'i's,

It wasn't a 'proper' band, just a group of interchanging musicians doing their best, some played with feeling – others not so convincingly. It didn't matter – they were all enjoying themselves.

Watching for a while, I noticed how individuals stepped down from the stage to give up their place and allow someone else to have a go, but like the 2'i's, few of them got paid, and there was only one 'regular' group who preferred to play together. These 'regular' musicians were on stage as I came in – the 'wannabes' were in a queue in front of the stage with me.

Naturally I looked to see if Tony Sheridan was around, but he wasn't. It felt good to be so close to the musicians on stage, with their amplifiers placed up on chairs: blaring out only a few feet away from the front row, and so loudly that it was almost impossible to hear what the singers were singing about. This didn't bother the guitarists at all. Each competed with the other to create what was now a tremendous and meaningless cacophony of sound that didn't fit in with the songs they played at all.

I squeezed my way ever closer to the front of the stage, as I had done in the 2 i's, (careful not to upset anyone and thereby cause a fight) I was now as close as I could get to the stage, where I could see everything going on, and may now be able to learn something by watching the guitarists play.

On stage were Cos and Zom (both guitarists) and Ray Duval on drums (who set a world record for the longest non-stop drum solo) and there was also a third guitarist whose name I didn't know. But this person was the one who changed my life: without him ever knowing it, and was responsible for me later playing alongside Tony Sheridan. It was a miracle how it came about and puzzles me to this day. Maybe it was meant to be.

As I said, I was standing in front of the stage: wanting to be as close as possible to the band. It was a great atmosphere and I shall never forget the noise and heat of the place. Maybe Tony Sheridan will turn up, and if he did, it would make my evening even better. But there was no sign of him, nor did I expect him to be there as no one had seen him around either. He was probably still on tour.

Then it happened, and no one could have planned it better. It was to open up a new career for me in music, even though nothing of the sort had been planned or even thought about. I wasn't looking to play in a band. I honestly didn't think I was good enough.

Quite unexpectedly, the guitarist on stage playing nearest to where I was standing, turned to me and shouted above the noise;

'Hey man! do you play?' I looked around me to see who he was talking to, but he was definitely talking to me. He looked uncomfortable, with a pained look on his face.

'Yea, a bit!', I shouted back, being careful not to tell him how little experience I had of playing in band.

'Can you take over for I while, I'm dying for a piss?'. And with that he quickly handed me his guitar and rushed off to the toilet.

'OK mate', I shouted after him, and climbed nervously up onto the stage, my mind racing: while the rest of the band stopped playing and watched – wondering who I was.

'What's your name?' shouted one of the band members, none of whom I had met before.

'Colin! I shouted back, they began playing all the songs I loved – with me joining in as best I could; some songs I knew and some I didn't. To cover up any mistakes I played quietly when I didn't know the chords, and loudly when I did. No one seemed to notice and no one cared: I knew I had a lot to learn: but was both keen and determined to catch up..

'Do you sing as well Colin?' It was 'Cos' the lead guitarist. I wasn't ready to sing, but didn't want to say no, just in case the band asked someone else to come up on stage to take my place.'Yea, a bit', I answered, at the same time sensing I was out of my depth. The whole band was now looking long and hard at me, waiting to make a start.

'OK, what are you going to sing then?' shouted 'Cos'. I felt this was my chance to make or break, sink or swim – believing this opportunity may never come my way again.

'Do you know 'Twenty flight rock?' I asked.

'Of course!' said the lead guitarist, 'Lets go!'
The band sprang into action and I sang the song as
best I could. After I had finished there was a
pregnant pause and then silence, my heart sank,
then everyone clapped loudly. It had gone down
well. Now more confident I sang a few more
songs; mostly Elvis numbers, again using the
same three chords in every one, hoping no one
noticed (although I'm sure the other musicians
did!) I could see them wincing out of the corner of
my eye, but no one criticised me; I began to love
it!

It was great playing in a band where no one
criticized anyone else. Everyone was there for the
joy of the music. I stayed and played until we
came to the end of that magical first evening, and
the guitarist, who I was standing in for, and had
gone to the toilet, never came back – I would
never see him again. Happy and flushed with

excitement, I merely leaned his guitar up against his amplifier and went home happy.

From then on, when home from the sea, I felt I could finally stop searching for Tony Sheridan; I had spent too much time looking for him, and was busy at the 'Top Ten' with my new-found friends. I hadn't forgotten about Tony – far from it. If I had known where he was playing, I would have dropped everything and gone to wherever it was in a flash.

The next time I was home I rushed back to the 'Top Ten', but this time carrying my very own electric guitar, having ditched the Spanish acoustic for a German 'Framus'; I also had my own amp, a tiny 'El Pico' but soon found out it was totally 'unfit for purpose'. It had no guts, but it was cheap! I thought I had arrived when I first bought it, but I was still a 'new boy', and the 'El

Pico' didn't do my image much good. But I always received a great welcome whenever I arrived back at the 'Top Ten'.

'Hi, Col, did you have a good trip? Where did you go this time?' and I would tell them all about it. The band had accepted me; I was one of them and it felt great.

But I saw the way they looked at my Tiny 'El Pico' amplifier, smirking at each other as they did so. How was I to know the El Pico was worse than useless? But I was to find out for myself. But we were all soon into the music again and nothing else mattered.

All the band members had their favourite songs and I learnt more about music in half an hour at the 'Top Ten' than I had learnt in four years at sea, and continued to learn, not only from the band, but from the visiting guitarists as well. If only Tony Sheridan would arrive and play, so that I could benefit from some of his magic too!

I was always flushed and excited whenever my ship came into the port of London and was soon rushing off again to the the 'Top Ten' to join my friends and having the time of my life. Music was now what I wanted to do most: the sea no longer held me spellbound.

That's what the new music did to many of us, and the fun of it was learning from each other. No one kept their talent to themselves. If someone played a clever riff, or a snazzy chord, we'd straight away ask, 'How did you do that?' and soon everyone was playing it.

The cellar clubs of London's Soho were not only the birthplaces of British rock 'n' roll, but schools of music too. In those early days there were no formal teachers of rock, no 'real' schools or places where you could pay someone to teach you this stuff.

Most of us learnt by listening to the American rock and roll records and the great black rhythm and blues artists, as well as some of the terrific country-music guitarists.

I had been away at sea too long and now wished I hadn't! Every band member benefited from being together with other musicians; No one cared how good you were – Doing it is the best way of learning it, and learning it is best done by doing it.

British bands had come a long way since Bill Haley first arrived in England. His music caused a riot in nearly every British city he visited. I know because I was there in London when it happened. We, the young, were in the grip of a revolution; whether that is really what it was or not didn't matter, but it certainly felt like it. Nothing like it happened again.

Police cars were being turned over in the streets

of London, near the Elephant and Castle, kids in the cinemas were dancing in the aisles to 'Rock around the Clock', where once they sat quietly in neat disciplined rows. For a for a while the police and other authorities, as well as parents and teachers, had lost control; That's how powerful the new music was.

It felt as if we, the young, were breaking out of an inner prison of rules and regulations: which had been stifling us for far too long, and now we had music – our music,which had come to set us free. I remember buying my first Elvis record and excitedly taking it home to my parents.

'Dad, listen to this!' I was sixteen at the time. I watched him and after a few seconds he looked up at me and I sincerely believed he was going to love it: but instead his eyes narrowed and before the record had finished playing he scoffed sarcastically; 'Turn it off, it's rubbish.' I couldn't believe it, how could he say that? The record was awesome! But despite my deep disappointment at the time; I was in a way glad the older generation didn't like the new music. At last the young had something of their our own. That's how we saw the 'rubbish', as my dad called it.

Now it belonged to us, maybe it always had, even though at first we hadn't realized it. There was no way the older generation would accept the new music. But we will continue to play these great rock 'n' roll numbers over and over again as long as we live, as others are doing all over the world as we speak. For us the music will never go away. It lift us up and fills our hearts, making our empty lives worth living.

Music has moved on now, as it has always does. Each generation is inspired by the music of their own times; as ours has done. 'The Beatles' were to take it on and soar with it to new heights. And their own music, though different from ours, will never go away.

Not for us the pre-rock sterile days of glitzy mirrored balls hanging from the posh ceilings of the Mecca and Locarno ballrooms, where once the young bucks and the pretty girls of London would go in the 50's – we were there only because there was nowhere else to go. We needed somewhere where we could all get together and be free.

It wasn't much fun in those snobbish ballroom places. There was no excitement, nothing interesting going on, just terribly boring big-band music and one big fashion show between 'mods' and 'rockers' – to see who wore the latest winkle picker shoes, or wore the shortest, bum-freezer Italian jackets, or the latest hairstyle. While in the other corner, the 'rockers' showed off their 'bumper' style 'creeper' shoes' and knee-length

Edwardian jackets and their 'DA' (duck's arse) hairstyles. This fashion competition lasted well into the 60's but again, how boring is that? Thankfully the 'mods' wouldn't be seen dead in the dingy cellar-clubs of Soho.

2. HAMBURG

The incredible Hamburg trip was where we first met The Beatles – It came about while I was once more home from the sea and playing again at the 'Top Ten' in London's Soho. It was June 1960. At that time it was common for bands to be randomly put together in the cellar clubs by promoters working for the many holiday camps, looking for musicians and singers to provide low cost entertainment for the visiting holidaymakers. The camps were also good places for amateur entertainers to gain 'show-biz' experience, and many went on to become famous.

As a result the cellar clubs of Soho became good hunting grounds for any new talent.

I had also once been offered a six-week 'summer season' as a singer at a holiday camp by a Butlins promoter, but couldn't take it, as I was then still in the Merchant Navy.

But this time it was different; I had now left the sea, having seen much of the world on my many different ships. It was time to move on, I now had a new interest and this time it

was music. There were many more experiences to have, and more of my life to be lived. I was still only twenty. And during all this time at sea I had never forgotten Tony Sheridan.

I was there in the 'Top Ten' club when Ian Hines: a well-known rock pianist on the scene in

London, was asked to put a band together on behalf of a German club owner named Bruno Koschmieder. Herr Koschmieder was looking for something exciting to take to his club in Hamburg. He had heard about the bands playing in London's Soho and hoped to find a English band to play for him and also bring the young Germans something new.

I had just finished playing for the evening and the 'Top Ten' was quickly emptying; The teenage audience was rushing off to the many parties in the area. Ian Hines came over to me just as I too was about to leave the club and join the partying. I was surprised when he asked,

'Colin, how would you like to play in Hamburg for seventeen days?' I was taken aback,

'I don't know, tell me more'. It sounded very interesting.

'I've been approached by this German guy, he's

looking for an English band to play at one of his clubs in Hamburg. I'm putting a band together, do you fancy it?' I thought about it;

'How much is he paying?' I didn't really need the money, but I was always up for doing something a bit different – and money always helps!

'Twenty pounds, plus free accommodation and fares, are you interested?'

I did a quick calculation; twenty pounds was a lot of money in those days, I could buy a new suit for that when I got back home to London! I already knew a bit about Hamburg, having been there on a ship that called there on its way to Sweden. I always remembered Hamburg as being a lively city, with plenty going on, but at that time our ship only stayed for a short while. But the more I thought about playing there, the more I liked the idea. It would be cool being a part of the first English rock 'n' roll band to play in Germany.

'OK Ian, count me in'.

'You're going then?'

'Yes, I'm in – who else is up for it?'

'Don't know yet, Col, but thanks, I'll let you know when I've got everyone together and we'll meet in the 'Freight Train' cafe to work out the travel arrangements and passports.'

We had no worries about the reception we would get in Germany in 1960: even though the war had been over only a relatively short time ago, and there was still plenty of bomb damage left in London to remind us of what had happened. Many British families had lost someone injured or killed, as mine had, and my school,was also two thirds destroyed. But as far as most of the youth of England was concerned this stuff was in the past.

It didn't mean these horrific things were forgotten, they couldn't possibly be, but the youth of the world is no different from our own, and we all needed to get some fun back into our lives, and rock 'n' roll is what gave it to us.

The first meeting of those who had agreed to go was arranged. The band was to be called the 'Jets' – a name given to all the bands put together by the organiser Ian Hines, who was also going to join us on the trip to Germany.

We met in the 'Freight Train', a cafe in Berwick Street (on the first or second of June 1960). I didn't know any of the other band members who were there that day as Cos, Zom and Ray Duval, the ones I had played with at the 'Top Ten', had turned down the offer and were not coming. Which was a pity really, as we all fitted in so well together as a band.

The first thing those that were going needed to do was to arrange our own passports; I collected mine from the passport office in London on 3rd

June 1960.We then all met again at the 'Freight Train' for a final briefing, but by then there were serious problems. It looked like some of those who had agreed to go to Hamburg were having second thoughts, and not everyone showed up. Even the organiser, Ian Hines, didn't come.

More seriously we had no drummer, nor a lead guitarist, and the trip looked unlikely.

It was a disaster for those of us waiting to go; we had collected our passports and said our goodbyes to our families . We had been given directions to the 'Kaiser Keller' in Hamburg, where we were to play, together with our tickets for the crossing from Harwich to the Hook of Holland, leaving the following day, the 4th of June. But two of the most important members of the band were missing. No band can play rock music without a drummer or a lead guitar. It looked like the 'Jets' wouldn't be going anywhere.

Those of us who were ready to go sat down with our cappuccinos and waited for Ian Hines to come and sort it all out, but he never arrived, nor did the drummer and nor did the lead guitarist. We knew we couldn't go to Hamburg with only half a band. We waited and waited, until we were certain the two main band members wouldn't be coming, and still Ian Hines, the organiser, hadn't shown up. We heard he was trying to find replacements for the missing drummer and lead guitarist. It was a bad start and a deathly hush descended on the once eager, new band members. But there was was nothing we could do about it.

'I can play drums a bit,' said Jimmy Ward an Irish boy, who was to be the main singer and also keyboard player, 'We can borrow a drum kit when we get there'.

The rest of us sat there in silence, not at all convinced by what Jimmy was suggesting.

'We'll still need a lead guitarist, Jimmy!' said someone else, and I wondered if this great trip was ever going to happen. All the signs were that it was dead in the water.

We were supposed to be boarding the train leaving for Germany the following day. But that's when the second part of the miracle I told you about earlier was about to happen.

'Tony Sheridan is free and back from his tour with Eddie Cochran and Gene Vincent' said someone. I was stunned and now all ears – he was the one I had been searching for all this time in Soho! Didn't someone also tell me he was on tour with Gene Vincent and Eddie Cochran? Is there really a chance he could be coming with us? I got quite excited: it would be fantastic if he did come, but as I didn't know anyone present, I decided to wait and see.

The waiting seemed like an eternity – why don't

they make up their minds and agree to take Tony Sheridan with us? But for some unknown reason no one wanted to take him.

'Oh No, not him!' said one of those waiting to go – It was Rick Hardy the singer/guitarist, one of the few who had been paid to sing at the 2'i's club. There was obviously some bad blood between Tony and Rick. In fact I was later told they disliked each other intensely.

Both sang at the 2'i's and Rick Hardy later told me he had 'kicked Tony's guitar in', when Tony was standing in front of the stage at the 2'i's waiting to come on. It was while waiting that Tony had insulted and provoked Rick while he was still on stage singing. Tony demanded Rick got off the stage, as it was now Tony's turn to sing, but Rick wasn't yet ready to give up his place.

Rick told me later that this was why he had

kicked out at Tony and smashed his guitar.

They still didn't like each other, and at the meeting in the 'Freight Train' it appeared nothing had changed. Rick Hardy didn't want to work with Tony Sheridan, and it was no surprise when Rick later left the 'Jets' for southern Germany, where he made a solo record, which was to be the first rock record ever made in Germany by a British rocker.

Back at the 'Freight Train' someone asked, 'Who else can we get at short notice?' But all the lead guitarists suggested by the band were already playing elsewhere, and others were on tour. No one knew anyone talented enough, and available, there was only Tony Sheridan.

I was really keen that they would take him, despite Rick Hardy's strong opposition to having Tony in the 'Jets'. But I was biased and couldn't wait to meet Tony and talk to him, and most of all to play alongside him. I had never forgotten the first time I heard him play and how deeply his playing and singing had affected me.

My inner voice was shouting, 'Take him!, Take him!, but not everyone was keen on doing so and I was mystified. Why not? He's great! Obviously they knew more about him than I did. I began to fear the worst – that the whole Hamburg idea would be called off. But not everyone was yet ready to throw in the towel. A long period of silence followed: no one was able to come up with any new ideas.

'It looks like Tony Sheridan is the only one free and we're leaving for Germany early tomorrow morning, does anyone know where we can contact him?' It was Jimmy asking.

'I know where he is,' said someone else, 'I'll go and get him now, I won't be long.' It was agreed by everyone, except Rick Hardy, but he begrudgingly went along with the others, even though it meant working with Tony Sheridan. If Rick knew of another lead guitarist available he would have nominated him, but he didn't, and we were running out of time.

I couldn't wait to see Tony again and finally confirm it really was the same person I had admired for so long, but hadn't met. He was by far the best singer/guitarist I had ever heard. The band member looking for Tony finally came rushing back.

'Yes, he's coming.' he spluttered, out of breath. It is what I had been waiting for. Not only did we now have a band for Hamburg, but a band with Tony Sheridan in it! All we needed now was for a drum kit to be sorted out for Jimmy Ward when we got to Hamburg.

But there was a long delay before Tony finally arrived – during which time none of us could keep still. The waiting for Tony became unbearable, but delay, and lack of concern for organisation, was to become Tony Sheridan's trademark, and it had already cost him a future with the BBC TV music shows.

We waited and waited, everyone shuffling around, some nervously tapping their fingers on the table, until Tony, at last arrived – much later than we had expected. He walked casually in and looked around at everybody, as if the place belonged to him. I was captivated afresh and completely spellbound. Rick Hardy was the first to respond, sneering;

'Bloody typical, he's late again.' Rick made no effort to hide his resentment at seeing Tony Sheridan appear. Tony ignored him. But inside I was ecstatic and it was difficult to hide.

It's him! It's him! I shouted to myself; The one I had been looking for all this time!

Of course I recognized him straight away and was

unable to hide my joy – I was like a dog with two tails! To think that he and I will be playing together in the same band was beyond my comprehension. I couldn't hide how I felt for him from the rest of the band.

Doubts set in, I didn't really know if I was going to be good enough to play alongside Tony, but quickly reassured myself with the thought that I had been chosen for the band, and shouldn't put myself down – I was there as the 'Jets' rhythm guitarist and singer – end of story.

But clearly not everybody was as happy about Tony as I was. Some looked at me strangely as if to say; What's he so pleased about? I had no idea why they showed so much ill will towards such a great talent – but I didn't know the whole story. I had been away at sea and not heard about Tony and the things he did, which may have explained their hostility towards him. He had also kept everyone waiting, which felt like a sign of contempt.

Meanwhile I was still thinking what a great band this was going to be! But right now, Tony sat at a table by himself, as I did – not knowing anybody. The atmosphere in the room was one of nervous tension, bordering on anger towards Tony Sheridan. The other band members sat together at one table, talking almost in whispers, while I still sat by myself, having still not been introduced to anyone. They were all strangers to me.

All was not well, not just with Rick Hardy and Tony, but surprisingly amongst some of the others too, which I didn't expect. They were not pleased to have Tony Sheridan with them. Was it jealousy? Was it because he was a greater talent than they were? I don't know.

It was while the others were quietly talking to

each other, that Tony came over to me. We didn't know each other of course, and I suspected he was coming to introduce himself.

He was tall and slim with a face that looked as though it had been about a bit, and endured a few disputes. He sat down and half smiled. It was quite a gentle smile and he spoke softly. Nothing like the loud, brash, rock 'n' roller I had first seen in the 2 'i's. cellar club so long ago.

'It's Colin isn't it?' and I wondered how he knew my name already. Maybe he had asked the other band members who else was going to Germany, and had been told about me.

'Yes', I said. 'And you're Tony Sheridan. You're coming with us to Germany, aren't you?' He frowned a bit before he spoke and then leaned forward so that the others, who were now looking at us, couldn't hear what he was about to say.

'Listen Colin', he said with a whisper, and put his arm round my shoulder, 'Why don't we leave these tossers here, and just me and you go to Hamburg together?' I couldn't believe it! Here he was, just arrived, had been given a job, and was now trying to wreck all the arrangements! It could have been that he didn't want to work with Rick Hardy.

I didn't even have to think about my answer, as he looked at me with wide eyes and a mischievous smile, waiting to hear what I would say. I admit I did feel a bit honoured that he wanted me to go with him and not anyone else, but I wasn't about to let him split up the band. It now looked to me as though his reputation was completely deserved.

'Sorry Tony I'm with them,' and getting up I walked over to join the others, leaving Tony at the table sitting by himself.

He sat there for a moment, still with the same

smile, before he, too, came over to join us, and in the conversations that followed between Tony and I, nothing more was ever said concerning the suggestion he made about leaving the other musicians behind. This was the first time I had spoken to Tony Sheridan and things were becoming clearer as to why, despite his talent, he was so unpopular with his fellow musicians.

But there are always two sides to a story and I hadn't heard Tony's side yet, bearing in mind, as I have already said, I spent most of my time away at sea and was a new boy on the London rock 'n' roll scene. But whatever Tony's reason was for suggesting we split up the band: it was clearly wrong, and there was no way I would have gone along with it.

Other than Rick Hardy's story, I didn't hear any others that explained Tony's terrible reputation for unreliability and confrontations, nor was I prepared to dig any deeper.

I decided it was better to stay out of any controversial conversations to do with all that stuff, and to make no comments of my own. I really didn't think it concerned me, and from my experiences of life at sea I knew that any banter like that will destroy a group of people quite quickly, especially as we will soon be living and working closely together.

Early the following morning, all the preparations having been made. Everyone carrying their passports and tickets: Tony Sheridan, Jimmy Ward, Peter Wharton, Rick Hardy and I boarded the train from London to Harwich, having waited as long as we could for Ian Hines to join us at the station – but he never arrived; We were now on our own.

We would not see Ian again until he arrived

later at the 'Top Ten' club, on the notorious Reeperbahn. Ian Hines never did explain why he didn't turn up and join us in London: when it was he who had organised the band for Hamburg! Ian was a quiet and secretive character.

During the crossing over the North Sea to the Hook of Holland I talked a lot with Tony Sheridan. He cut a lonely figure on deck looking out to sea, ignored by most of the band; he seemed to have a lot on his mind. We unexpectedly formed a strange bond. Strange because he and I were so unlikely to be friends. He was brash – but with moments of unexpected gentleness and sensitivity. He was also a great musician, as well as being an interesting and well educated guy, whereas I was none of these things.

There was hardly a topic Tony didn't have a personal point of view about, and in our long talks during the North Sea crossing, we found we had more in common than I thought. Apart from being born within a couple of months of each other in 1940, his father was of Irish extraction, and so was mine. His family on his mother's side was of Jewish descent and so was mine. He was from a family which included teachers, and so was mine.

The main difference between us was that while he regarded himself as Irish, and held an Irish passport, I saw myself as English (with Irish connections!) and held a British passport – feeling a strong loyalty to England: the country that had accepted my ancestors, sheltered them and educated them. But strangely there were other things we shared in our early lives.

When we were both sixteen, Tony had applied to go to sea and so had I, and in the same year! He had applied for officer training at the Royal Naval college at Dartmouth in the west of England, and I for training as an Able Seaman in the Merchant Navy, starting as a deck boy at the National Sea Training School at Sharpness, also in the west of England.

Tony told me how he was turned down by the Royal Navy when it was discovered he was colour blind, in red and green only, which is why he never held a drivers licence in the UK.

I was luckier than Tony; I was accepted for training in the Merchant Navy and saw much of the world on my nineteen different ships, and I did become an Able Seaman.

All our coincidences could be put down to pure chance, and probably meant nothing at all.

It depends on how you view them. Some may say that in our case it was fate that caused us to meet up with each other while treading the same pathway to music, and it was this that had brought us to the cellar clubs of Soho. But it was even simpler than that: We were brought together because we both loved the same kind of music; it was in London and Liverpool, where its impact on the young was greatest, and where all the early action began. British rock 'n' roll spread to other major cities of the UK and later to the whole world.

I remember being overwhelmed to have found, and even talking to, Tony Sheridan on a ship taking us to Hamburg, where unbeknown to us, Tony Sheridan and The Beatles impact would be greatly felt. There was much to ask Tony, and I wanted to get an idea as to who this talented boy really was. He told me about the 'Saints' his skiffle group, that had left Norwich during the night on the 'milk train' to seek fame and fortune in London's rock 'n' roll world. He had left a note with his sister, Kathy, to give to his mother, who would have tried to stop her son had she known what her talented son intended to do. She was sure to have had a 'better' career planned for him, after carefully overseeing his education for so long.

In London, Tony and his 'Saints' slept wherever they could, including benches in the London parks until they found a better place to stay. Their first accommodation was a pub in Seven Sisters Road, where in return for a bed, they played for the customers in the evening for free, and were each given a small amount of pocket-money.

But whatever forces were behind all the similarities in our backgrounds, they did help a lot to break down the barriers that could easily have existed between us, and once together, we would always remain the most unlikeliest of friends and even soul-mates. Yes, we argued, we fought, and disagreed, but nothing broke up our friendship.

My only regret is that in all the time we were together, I wasn't able to change him in any way – nor could anyone else. I would see many try and many fail. It was the fantastic women in his life who came closest to achieving it, as women are best equipped to decode and fathom out the frustrating yet uncomplicated minds of men! After escaping from his home he arrived in London where all the action was, and in an incredibly short period of time he became a force to be reckoned with in the unstable world of rock 'n' roll music. Tony was accepted by all who knew him and heard him play, as one of the best guitarist and singers in England.

Few could match him in technique, or the feeling he could put into his playing and singing. He was snapped up by British manager, Don Arden to accompany Eddie Cochran and Gene Vincent on their British and European tours.

Eddie was also regarded as one of the best guitarist/singers around, and together with Gene Vincent, both were already legends in England and both acknowledged Tony Sheridan's talent and wanted him with them on their UK tours.

Later on we were to meet up with other visiting American greats in the fabulous 'Star Club' in Hamburg, where we were resident band and re-named the 'Star Combo'. I lost count of the number of times I was asked why Tony didn't go to America: where he was sure to become a star. But he always dismissed these opportunities, which is something I was not able to understand until much later.

I was also there at the 'Star Club' when Tony was praised by the great Ray Charles who, while waiting in the wings to go on stage, had asked who the singer/guitarist was on stage at that time, and when told it was Tony Sheridan, Ray commented; 'He's good, very good'.

Other visiting American acts such as Joey Dee and the 'Starliters' (who once had Jimi Hendrix with them), tried to encourage Tony to seek his fortune in America. Joey Dee offered to help him by sponsoring him throughout the whole of America.

But Tony Sheridan wasn't seeking fame and fortune and he declined Joey Dee's offer,
But Joey and the 'Starliters' did accompany us with backing vocals on 'Ruby Baby' (one of the tracks on 'The Beatles First' LP) which our band recorded at Polydor Records in Hamburg with Tony Sheridan and the 'Jets', (renamed the 'Beat Brothers' by Polydor.)

Both In England and later in Hamburg, many tried to master Tony's technique.

In Hamburg it was George Harrison, John

Lennon, and Paul McCartney who were inspired by Tony Sheridan's talent and went out of their way to befriend him and learn from him (and succeeded). It was noticeable how John Lennon often stood on stage imitating Tony's stance.

Tony was happy to teach The Beatles – We all learnt from each other in those early days. He was in many ways unique, both in his playing style and his singing; there was no one like him at that time – until the new breed of hungry bands and talented singer/guitarists arrived on the scene to take his place and move things on – which included the talented 'Beatles', who choose to 'go it alone', moving on in a different direction. They had learnt what was current and changed it until it became their own original sound.

But let's go back to that first night at the 'Kaiser Keller' in Hamburg: where we had arrived tired and hungry. It was late in the afternoon and it was a long stressful journey from London via Harwich and the Hook of Holland, carrying all our gear.

The club was situated in the lively heart of St Pauli, the red-light district of Hamburg, similar to London's Soho. Both areas were notorious for their night-time entertainment and the many striptease clubs, brothels and clip-joints, all in close proximity to the more modest and traditional historic Hamburg theatres. We looked forward to a rest in our hotel and something to eat, but there was to be no rest, no hotel, and nothing to eat – instead we were to start playing that same night, and were taken down a wide marble staircase to the main hall. None of us at that time spoke any German but, luckily many young Germans spoke English, which most learnt at school.

At the bottom of the stairs was a reception desk and behind the desk was the 'Garderobe' (cloakroom). It was a small room with no lighting or windows. It was to serve as our accommodation for the duration of our stay. The gloomy room was a dump, and inside we could just about make out some bunk beds which had been pushed together to make room for us. It was a miserable place and not what we expected.

But in Germany musicians were treated no differently from any other club workers – there would be no 'star-status', and no special VIP treatment for us.

In the the massive main hall downstairs, next to our room, was a huge stage. It was much bigger than any stage we had played on before. We decided not to take any chances with the electrics and hurriedly made a quick check of the German power points to confirm that the amplifiers, microphones and all other electrical equipment was compatible with our own instruments and amplifiers, and was going to work. They all seemed to be OK.

The club was filling up fast with curious, excited teenagers, their bright, shining eyes and enthusiastic faces lined up like beacons in front of the stage, just watching and waiting for us to start. We didn't intend to let them down. There was a tense and feverish atmosphere on that first night in the 'Kaiser Keller' and we could all feel it. We sensed the audience felt what we ourselves were feeling. It was a strange mixture of anticipation and excitement.

The word had got round in Hamburg that the first English rock 'n' roll band to visit Germany was now at the 'Kaiser Keller'. Everyone was looking at us curiously, wondering if the 'Englander' were going to be any good or not – but we didn't know either, as we had never played together before, and there had been no time to practice.

It would be a totally new experience for all of us, including the audience – just because we were good individually, didn't mean we would be good together. We were about to see.

But from my own point of view, I knew that with Tony Sheridan in the band, all would go well, and I was confident that we would not just be 'good,' but 'very good'.

The young Germans already had their own pop stars: Ted Herold, (the German Elvis), Freddy Quinn, Heino and Peter Kraus. But Hamburg hadn't seen a 'live' British rock 'n' roll band yet, and we were keen to show them what we could do.

Still hungry, we had just enough time to rush out and buy a bowl of soup and a bread roll at 'Harold's Place' in the Grosse Freiheit, (the street outside the 'Kaiser Keller.) This upset the German club owner, Herr Koschmieder as he didn't know whether or not we were coming back. Tough! We were hungry, and found at least some food we liked, even if it was just soup and a roll: it would take a long while before we got used to any other German food. Now feeling much better, we rushed back to the club, just as a small search party of waiters came towards us, having been sent out to find us.

It was difficult getting back into the 'Kaiser Keller' on our return as the crowds were still pouring in. Once inside we climbed up on stage. The place was now packed with about five or six hundred people, maybe more, mostly teenagers. Every square metre of the hall was taken up. It was a great atmosphere, and we were now almost ready to play.

The main lights were dimmed except for those

at the entrance hall area, and the mixed coloured lights around the bars and stage, which stayed on permanently. The crowd grew quieter. I looked briefly at the other members of the band and could almost touch their tense, excited anticipation. None of us knew what to expect. The huge main bar at one end of the hall was now knee-deep in customers and the first large group of teenagers, who had earlier pitched a permanent camp in front of the stage, were still there and within touching distance of the band. None dared leave their place in case they couldn't get it back again.

There were far too few bar staff and waiters to cope with all the orders for drinks. The boss was making a killing; even though most of the youngsters were not interested in the drinks, and instead pushed and jostled each other to get as close to the band as they could, though all the best places had been taken up. The rows upon rows of eager faces had doubled in number. We felt good, knowing it was going to be quite a night!

The young fans were constantly pointing and analysing every move we made and then discussing it. All seemed to have a different opinions as to what it was we were doing.

Tony began what turned out to be his usual ritual of tuning and re-tuning his 'Martin' guitar before starting. This sometimes went on for ages; and during this time he completely ignored everything around him: the audience, the restless boss and everyone else. At times he held the whole guitar up to his ear; I wondered if he had done the same on the 'live' BBC TV shows, and imagined the producer pulling his hair out as Tony completely disrupted his carefully worked-out timing! I smiled to myself.

Once Tony had finished his own tuning he

turned to me. The expectant crowd was now hushed once more, expecting him to kick-off with the music, but he didn't.

'Colin, give me an 'E' which I did. He then asked me to do it again saying,

'Fuck me, that's well out of tune!' then came, 'Up a bit', down a bit', while all the while I fiddled with my rhythm guitar pegs as instructed. Tuning was not my strongest point and in those days I had no automatic tuner to help me.

I had arrived late on the music scene and had certainly not played in front of a large audience like this before. I knew I had to learn very quickly and Tony turned out to be an uncompromising teacher, as all of us found out when under his instruction.

'Down a bit more', until at last Tony was fairly happy. Meanwhile the audience waited.

'Let's hear the full chord now,' and Tony

winced as I gave him what he asked for.

'Where did you get that fucking thing from?' referring to my recently acquired second-hand 'Framus' guitar. I ignored Tony's insults. I liked it. It was a semi-acoustic cut-out model with a blond finish; the first and only electric guitar I ever owned. The tiny 'El Pico' amp I bought with me to go with it, was also the cheapest. That's all I could afford at the time.

On that first night Tony didn't ask Rick Hardy to tune up (they still weren't talking to each other.) After tuning Pete Wharton's bass guitar we were ready to go and still the audience was hushed. I could see the wide excited eyes of the youngsters closest to the stage were still firmly fixed on us. They were clearly fascinated; even though we hadn't played anything yet! It was like we were visitors from another planet.

I looked across the room and could see Herr

Koschmieder standing at the back of the hall, restlessly looking this way and that, then at us and his watch, and then over at us again: he was impatient to see what he was getting for his money. He had never heard us play either. Nobody had. Tony was ready at last and moved up to the microphone and began fiddling with the height adjustment until he was happy with that too.

During all this time he stoically and indifferently ignored the restless youngsters, and I wondered if he had kept the whole audience waiting deliberately, so as to heighten their anticipation, which was now at fever pitch, and could easily turn into annoyance.

It was time to get going and Tony turned to his Fender amplifier and fiddled quickly with the knobs, maybe he really wasn't playing games and did all this deliberately, maybe he needed to go through this ritual – It was a kind of warm-up and I found he always did this.

Tony turned round to us and I saw Rick Hardy sneering. Tony ignored him and stepped up to the mike. The audience was strangely hushed again as he turned round to us one last time, and whispered, 'Skinny Minny' and with nothing more being said he let rip with his guitar. It was an explosion of fierce and emotional sound, with the whole band following close behind. The hair on my neck stood up: in the same way it did when I first heard him play. The startled youngsters in front of the stage, took a step back, completely shocked by the ferocity of the sound that hit them.

Tony's guitar screamed out in agony as he hopped and twisted across the stage, his face a picture of torment and superhuman effort, sending constant shivers of excitement up and down my spine. The band, which had stuttered a bit at first, soon caught up with him and we were all playing together – sounding like one tight unit.

The young German audience, at first stunned, looked at each other, never having seen or heard anything like Tony before. Then, unable to keep still, and as if guided by some hidden signal, they all rushed towards the centre of the dance floor and were soon bobbing and kicking as they wildly danced in their unique Hamburg style of Rock 'n roll. No one danced better than they did. It was wild yet graceful, structured yet full of innovation and variation.

The Kaiser Keller was now one teeming, writhing mass of young humanity, and even the waiters were joining in: dancing alongside the youngsters. But my cheap little 'El Pico' amplifier was screaming out, farting and burping and distorting badly, unable to sustain the power I was trying to put through it.

'Turn that fucking thing off!', shrieked Tony above the din: unable to stand my little amp making such rude noises directly behind him. I now played acoustic, but my Framus guitar made no impact, as Tony followed his first number with more of his favourite rock songs. Playing without an amp meant I might as well not be playing at all. No one could hear me.

Fortunately it didn't make any difference whether I played or not, as it now looked as though none of the rest of us were going to get a look-in, and sing a few numbers ourselves, but that didn't matter either. Tony was doing a great job on his own, and didn't want to stop.

Flushed with a strong sense of satisfaction, that the first night was going so well, we carried on playing late into that first night, and everyone was happy.

Bruno Koschmieder was beaming, and the crowd was in ecstasy. Clearly it was right to let Tony carry on, and in the end each of us did manage to make a contribution and sing before the evening finally came to an end. It was a truly fantastic experience, something we would never forget. Nor would the young Germans. But my 'El Pico' never recovered from the pounding it took on that first night and it was 'binned', in order to put it out of its misery, and Tony out of his as well. He was glad to see the back of the El Pico. I borrowed a better, more substantial amplifier until I could build my own, and the problems went away.

Happily for me; but sadly for my mate, Peter Wharton, our bass player had to leave the band and go back to England due to illness. I spoke to Tony: suggesting I take over bass and told him I was prepared to buy a bass guitar, provided he taught me how to play it.

He agreed straight away and I took over Peter's job as bass guitarist and bought my first bass (a 'Hofner' violin type) from 'Steinway', the famous piano maker, whose store was in the centre of Hamburg. Tony taught me all I needed to know about playing bass guitar.

I took to it like a kangaroo takes to hopping, and with Tony's help I soon mastered it. Tony's only advice was, 'Keep it simple, work with the drums, and always remember, I'm the lead guitarist!' (he hated busy bass players!). After a while, during those first crazy nights at the 'Kaiser Keller', Jimmy, Rick and I got the chance to sing regularly and although Jimmy was doing well on drums, he couldn't sing and play drums well at the same time. He did try, and he had a great voice, but the 'Jets' badly needed a permanent drummer.

Tony was unquestionably the star in Germany –

as he was in England, and deservedly so. The audiences just couldn't get enough of him, and we were all having a terrific time. They were wild, crazy days, and we didn't want them to end. But worried that at any time we would see the Hamburg police arrive and close the place down as alcohol was being sold after ten pm, and juveniles were present in the bars.

But this was Hamburg, and the laws were different to those in England: We could drink all night if we wanted to! But in Germany, juveniles under seventeen were not even allowed to be out after ten pm in any of the clubs and bars. If they were found, they would be arrested, their parents contacted and told to collect them from the police station. Which, of course, didn't please the parents. After playing long into the night, and at the end of each incredible evening, we would join the bar staff and waiters for a drink.

The German girls who stayed behind with us were beautiful and friendly, and all our drinks were being paid for. Eventually we would drag ourselves back to the Garderobe and flop onto our bunks. Some of the girls tried to go with us, but after the long night, we were far too drunk, or too tired to pay them much attention. One girl named Gerda climbed into my bunk and I had to ask her politely to leave (an opportunity I had never turned down in my life before!). But there is something attractive about a boy who plays in a band, and whatever it is, it worked for us, and also for the girls.

The nights at the 'Kaiser Keller' got better and better and just as wild as the first: even more people came in – having heard about us from others. But I was soon to see another side to Tony Sheridan. Fights were going on and we couldn't play while bottles were flying over our heads.

There are only so many times we could duck our heads while playing.

On one particular night it developed into a full-scale battle, which raged between two large opposing groups: The 'halbstarke' (young trouble makers) and the waiters. Tables, chairs and bottles were being thrown around and people were getting hurt. It was a dangerous situation. The band was unable to do anything but stop and watch the fight.

It turned out to be a good one, a bit like something out of the wild west days. The safest thing for us to do was to stay on the stage and protect our equipment, but this passive approach was not for Tony Sheridan. He was up for anything, including a good fight.

The Irish in him came out, and he wanted to take part in what was going on. He carefully put down his guitar and jumped headlong into the fighting and heaving throng of bodies on the dance floor and was soon giving as good as he got. Wisely the rest of us decided to stay out of it. Some shows are better to watch than to take an active part in.

The club manager, a bullish, ugly man, named Willy, was also in the thick of it, and soon became a prime target for the young 'halbstarke' while Bruno Koschmieder, the owner, was nowhere to be seen. He had obviously 'done a runner' and retreated to his office.

We watched as the yobbos continued throwing the chairs at Willy until he was completely buried beneath a pile of chairs so high that they almost reached the club ceiling.

Willy was somewhere underneath, but no longer visible. I had never seen anything like it in my life, not even in all my sea-going days, when big fights were common. As I watched, more and more chairs were being thrown on top of him. But Willy took the wisest option; staying exactly where he was – buried but safe. The trouble went on for quite a while and most of the the peaceful youngsters, who were just looking for a night out, hid in the toilets.

When it at last looked like it had all quietened down, and the mess had been cleared up, it started again when a young German fan came to the stage and politely asked Tony to play 'Good Golly Miss Molly'. The young German boy meant no harm as he stood there looking up at Tony, wide-eyed and waiting for an answer, and of course,completely unaware what Tony's response might be. But sadly for the youngster, Tony was still in 'fight' mode.

'I don't fucking like 'Good Golly Miss Molly' and much to our amazement jumped off the stage and punched the young fan in the mouth. The whole band was shocked, as there was no need for it, and once again a big fight started, and again there was no shortage of people wanting to get involved and calling themselves 'fans'.

The world is full of mindless morons, you will find them everywhere, their idea of fun is to spoil the enjoyment of others, due to their own warped inability to have fun themselves. How sad is that? As for Tony punching the youngster merely for making a request, it was something I still don't understand to this day. What could he possibly get out of doing something like that? I really had no idea why he did it.

Peace was restored when an army of waiters from nearby clubs rushed in to help their neighbours, armed with coshes and knuckledusters. Some wore leather gloves with the fingers parts cut out to protect their knuckles, others carried horse whips or home-made batons. All would wade in quickly to regain control. Those yobbos that hadn't escaped from the club were rounded up and given a good kicking before being ejected.

The police were rarely called. This was St Pauli: where the clubs solved their own problems: mainly by helping each other when trouble started, and when the trouble was too big for a single club to handle on its own.

Luckily Tony was back on stage with no serious injuries, but this would not always be the case, and he was to learn his lesson – street-fighting is dangerous, and often turns nasty.

Tony got himself into serious trouble when a tendon in the middle finger of his right hand was severed by a beer glass during a confrontation in a bar; his finger was so badly damaged that he would never able to bend it again.

Later publicity photographs showing him playing guitar also show the permanently straight middle finger of Tony's right hand. If it had been the middle finger on his left hand it would have been far worse, as it would have seriously affected his ability to shape the chords. He would then have been forced to play left-handed. In our quieter moments I asked Tony why he fought without having a good reason. He would just smile and never answer.

Tony's first girlfriend in Hamburg was Liane – a lovely, quiet, blond-haired girl, but it didn't last long, for reasons only Liane and Tony would be able to say. I didn't ask why.

Rosie was Tony's first real love in Germany and she, too,was and still is, a great girl, as was Monica and Anna. They saw more in Tony than many other girls could see. Tony cared about his own Norfolk family, too, although he rarely saw them. Family and relationships are often the prices to be paid for fame and success. They are incompatible worlds and there are very few artists who can make them work as one. I never asked Tony about his family. It was something private and he rarely talked about his early life.

Morality in the 60's was just a matter of choice. We were left to make our own decisions about right and wrong, and we didn't always make the 'right' ones. But again the kind of life we led made long-lasting relationships almost impossible.

The other members of the band all found girlfriends too. I was later told by a German friend (Fritz) that some of his fellow waiters, secretly resented the way the German girls were 'throwing themselves' at the English guys. That was their problem; we could have been any nationality, that's what boys and girls do. Why pick on the English? I found out later the real problem was that unknown to the band, some of the waiters were already going out with some of the girls, who were being far too friendly towards us.

Finding the right food in Hamburg is always difficult. German food is not the same as ours and we just wanted somewhere we could go for a 'proper' cooked meal: one that resembled English food. We were fed up with making do with soup, hamburgers or 'wurst' and didn't intend to eat that stuff forever. We longed for a proper roast dinner.

As a last resort we did go to the British Seaman's Mission, close to the Hamburg docks, where we could get some sort of English food, even if it was just baked beans on toast, or a fried egg sandwich and a nice cup of English tea. But it was too far to go and be back in time to play each evening.

Then a German friend told Tony and me about a great restaurant on the Reeperbahn: which we must try. It was only minutes away from where we played. We decided to give it a go, and sure enough it was a great place: very clean, with white tablecloths. It was a proper restaurant rather than a 'burger bar'. The entrance was down a small flight of steps leading from the Reeperbahn. We sat together at one of the cosy little tables by the window. The waiter, a very polite man, came over to us, bringing the menus with him.

After checking what most of the the stuff on the menu was, we happily placed an order for a large juicy steak each, with boiled potatoes, peas and gravy.

When the meal arrived, and we saw the great-looking steaks, we were really pleased. It was just like the Sunday dinners we had at home!. It tasted delicious and we ate the lot. This was now to be our favourite eating place and we became regulars there for a while. Then something shocking happened which spoiled it all.

While Tony and I were about to go out together again for a meal at the same place, we told a German friend about this great restaurant we were going to just around the corner, and where we were now regulars. He casually said,

'So you like horse meat do you? It stopped us in our tracks.

'What!' said Tony – not sure if the friend was joking, or we hadn't heard him correctly.

'Horse meat! You like it do you? I know this restaurant, it's famous for its great horse steaks.' We were both shocked and a bit sickened by what he told us.

'Is that what we've been eating?' and we looked at each other. Shocked.

'Of course, why, what's wrong with it?'. The friend looked puzzled by the fuss we were making, having no idea that in England we didn't eat horse meat.

'We don't eat horses in England!' said Tony, gruffly, as if it was our German friend's fault that we were eating there. I never saw Tony look so pale. He was now in 'pre-fight' mode.

'Why not? It tastes good.' said the friend, who was looking even more puzzled: especially as we had already eaten at this restaurant before, and had told him how good it was.

'In England its illegal to sell horse meat for humans to eat!' I said, now joining in, hoping to placate Tony, who was now getting really angry and I was keen to calm him down.

'That's why we don't eat dogs either, both are friends of humans', added Tony sullenly.

Our German friend walked away shaking his

head, then stopped and looked back,

'You 'Englander' are so difficult to understand!'

It was back to soup and 'wurst' again. Strangely, Tony and I, and others, too, had been happy to eat at this restaurant, so what was our problem? What was it that put us off eating horses? I really didn't know.

Back at the 'Kaiser Keller' skulduggery was afoot, and among the teenage revellers there was a group of men, shady-looking hard-cases, who sat together round several tables, close to the stage. They definitely looked out of place in the 'Kaiser Keller' – being much older men. Tony was spending more time with them and they had been in the club before.

I had no idea what was up; But something concerning us was definitely happening.

The last thing we expected was news that we

must leave the 'Kaiser Keller'.

3. 'REEPERBAHN'

Who knows what goes on in the cut-throat corridors of the club world? The word on the street was that Bruno Koschmieder, the owner of the 'Kaiser Keller, had been made an 'offer he couldn't refuse', and must let our band go. He had become too successful and now the big boys were moving in to cut themselves a slice of the rock 'n' roll cake.

We (the 'Jets') together with the waiters, arrived

to renovate the old hippodrome-type building which was a dump. It hadn't seen a customer for many years. It was to be named the 'Top Ten' after the cellar club in London of the same name, where most of the 'Jets' had played. It was a name I had suggested.

The new 'Top Ten' had a strange history. It once had a circus-like ring in the centre of a large hall, where horses trotted around inside the circle. On the outside of the ring were tables and chairs where people sat and watched the horses and where coffee was served!

But all this strange behaviour had long since gone out of fashion, and now a new purpose was found for the old building – which was totally different from the previous one. It was now to be a rock 'n' roll club!

The Eckhorn family who owned it, had hit bad times and needed a project to get them earning money. Rock 'n' roll fitted the bill. We worked hard on the renovation and even enjoyed it. The mountain of rubbish was cleared away and a stage was built. I believe Tony, (using his talent as an ex Norwich Art student,) painted a mural at the back of the stage and after a lot more hard work, the new club was ready.

I must say it looked really good. It didn't seem possible to have completed it in such a short time, and in early July we all moved in to our new accommodation above the apartment of Peter Eckhorn and his family. It was much more acceptable than the 'Garderobe' in the 'Kaiser Keller where we had lived before; We now had 'proper' beds and a lot more privacy.

On the flight of stairs leading up to our rooms was another apartment where 'Mutti' lived. (it was the name we called her by and means, 'mum' in

English). She was the house cleaner and lived alone in an apartment close to ours. She must have been about eighty years old, and a good woman. She helped to keep our rooms clean, although she didn't need to do it.

She had lived in her apartment for many years rent free and in return she did the cleaning for the Eckhorns. I liked her a lot, although I knew she was shocked by our behaviour – especially when she saw the band running around semi-nude in the apartment: with female visitors present! But this was the 60's!

Our first night on stage at the new 'Top Ten' was an instant success. It was full from the very beginning and looked fresh and modern. Most of our fans had followed us from the 'Kaiser Keller', which couldn't have made Bruno Koschmieder very happy, as his place was now virtually empty.

But the 'upside' was that our move away from the 'Kaiser Keller' made way for the the Liverpool bands:and allowed The Beatles to take our place there.

Later, Ringo Starr, then out of work, was to join the 'Jets' at the 'Top Ten' as our drummer, before returning to Liverpool and joining The Beatles (more about Ringo later).

Bruno Koschmieder was to get his revenge on whoever was responsible for causing us to move out of the 'Kaiser Keller' and into the 'Top Ten' – someone had tipped off the Hamburg Immigration Police that we were in Germany illegally, and early one morning, just after daybreak, we woke up to the sound of the door to our apartment being smashed in.

Five official-looking men wearing black leather ankle-length coats had forced their way in and began shouting and raving at us to get up, reminding me of stories from the bad old days when the SS were 'top dogs'. But these people were from the 'Auslaender Polizei', who dealt with matters to do with foreigners living and working in Germany.

The problem was we didn't have permission to stay or work in Germany. Neither club owner (Peter Eckhorn nor Bruno Koschmieder), had bothered to sort this out before we arrived. The men in black, (who still hadn't told us who they were), continued ranting and raving, 'Schnell', 'Schnell', 'Aufstehen!' (quick quick, get up!) which only pissed us off, and made us move more slowly. Once ready we were told to bring our passports with us and taken to the 'Davids Wache' (a police station on the Reeperbahn), where we were placed in detention.

Tony took it all in his stride, it wasn't the first

time he'd been arrested. None of us knew who had brought the police to our door, but you didn't need to be Miss Marple to identify the culprit. We were kept in police detention all day and interrogated: When did we arrive? who employed us?, how long did we intend to stay?

Then, late in the day, the top police boss came to see us. He was a man in his late 60's and walked with a stick. He interviewed us, one at a time, in private. Firstly he spoke to Tony, who later told me the two of them (he and the boss) had got on very well; Tony sometimes had this effect on people in authority. He could turn the charm on and off at will.

When my turn came the police boss said,

'You are in Germany illegally, but as I said to Mr Sheridan-McGinnity, we don't intend to bar you from coming here. If you leave now and return to England you can apply to the German

Embassy in London and obtain an 'Aufenthalts Erlaubnis' which allows you to enter and stay in Germany for a limited period. But first you will need to sign this form which says you agree to be deported.' He showed me the form he had already prepared.

He looked at me intently, and I wondered if Tony had been asked to sign the form as well.

'Does this form also say that if successful I can return and play in Hamburg?' I asked him.

'No, it means you agree to be deported; The rest will be dealt with by the German Embassy after making their enquiries.' I thought about it for a while and wasn't happy,

'If it doesn't mean I can come back and play here then I won't sign it.'

With that the boss's mood changed; He was angry. It had been a long day and he wanted the matter settled. I learnt later that Rick Hardy had already signed the form and agreed to be deported, but Tony and I, as well as other band members, had not. The boss then got up to leave, turning to me as he did so,

'Then you will stay here until we decide what to do with you.' After leaving us to rot until the very end of the day, the police boss visited us again.

This time he was no longer insisting we sign the form. The new deal was that we leave Germany voluntarily: without the stigma of a deportation stamp in our passports and once we got back to England we were to apply to the German Embassy in London for a visa.

We didn't trust the police boss: believing that the 'Auslaender polizei' in Hamburg would simply contact the German Embassy in London and tell them to refuse us entry into Germany. To counter this we had a cunning plan.

Instead of going back to London, we would go

to Holland and apply for permission to enter Germany at the German Embassy in Amsterdam: hoping they had no idea we had been arrested in Hamburg. It would take a couple of days, and we needed some money, as we were running short. Luckily we had the support of German friends who insisted they take us by car to Amsterdam and help in whatever way they could while we were there.

Someone suggested 'busking' in the Amsterdam streets to earn some money. Everyone was up for it except me; 'Busking' is too much like begging. But other unemployed English musicians had 'busked' in the streets, or in the passenger tunnels of the London underground stations. It was warm there and the acoustics helped their voices and even made their guitars sound better; It was like a ready-made sound studio!

For the sake of the majority I did finally go

along with it, but still found it embarrassing when sitting on the pavement in the main Amsterdam shopping district like a tramp, smiling and strumming my guitar, accepting whatever money the people passing by were prepared to give us. It worked, and people did give us money; But not much. It would have taken us a long time – probably all our lives, to get rich playing in the streets of Amsterdam!

The following day we returned to the German Embassy where we collected our visas, no questions asked, and were now granted entry to Germany for a limited period of time – on condition we register with the Auslaender Polizei in Hamburg. This we did and were each granted a work permit which we needed to renew regularly.

No questions were asked by the Hamburg Police as to how we got our visas. They must have realized what had happened on seeing the

Amsterdam visa stamps in our passports.

After that there were no more problems. Tony was pleased, and so was I. It was good to be back in Hamburg: where all the band had German friends and girlfriends, and they, too, were worried as to whether we would ever come back and play again.

Back at the newly-opened 'Top Ten' club the boss, Peter Eckhorn, although a lovely man, had illusions of grandeur and was insisting we all wear silly uniforms on stage – he forgot we were a rock 'n' roll band and not a posh orchestra.

This meant that at the 'Top Ten' we were all playing in Tartan jackets and neatly pressed trousers. And instead of my bass-guitar, I was given an orchestra-sized double bass on a stand. Mr Eckhorn thought it added to the 'ambience' of the club, but it didn't work. The double bass had no volume controls or pick-ups, which made it useless: especially when it came to playing the kind of music we played, not only did we look 'silly,' but sounded silly too.

The problem with managers, agents and club owners in the 60's was that few of them had any idea what rock 'n' roll music was all about: although it wasn't 'rocket science'.

There was a 'generation gap', but Peter Eckhorn finally saw the light and left us to it. He did insist that we all wore white shirts. Sure enough, once we got rid of the ridiculous uniforms, and the double bass, the music took off straight away. More people came in and now the 'Top Ten' looked a bit more like a rock 'n' roll club and was always full. We all loved it at the 'Top Ten' and every evening Tony would put on a great show. Other musicians came from far and wide to see him. This time, instead of all teenagers, the club started to fill up with the young, and not so young. It was OK as our music was meant for everyone.

At first, Tony didn't disappoint them: except when performing one of his more bizarre acts while singing a marathon version of 'What'd I say', which usually ended up with Tony, on a high, rolling off the stage and into the audience: while still singing and playing. He always managed to do it without breaking his guitar, which always fascinated me. It was such a difficult thing to do!

'What'd I say' would go on for an hour or so, and would finish with Tony lying prostrate under one of the customers tables or among some chairs, twitching and mumbling: so that no one knew whether he was having a seizure and about to die, or this was just part of his act. I don't think Tony knew either. He was 'out of it' and definitely 'on' something.

Those of us who had seen it all before simply ignored him. It was strange, but also quite sad to watch someone you admired acting so strangely. It wasn't as if he was copying someone else's act! The problem was he repeated the same thing again and again.

It wasn't long before no one took any notice of him as he lay there under a customer's table. The regular customers either ignored him or laughed and joked about it, while other newly- arrived customers watched in horror. What is he doing? What's it all about? Is he on drugs? Is this the Tony Sheridan we were told about?

Ever since I had known Tony, I have never seen him take drugs, although I knew he took stimulants. His behaviour led any fool to assume he was on something more and we all saw the drug dealers pestering him. It angered me to see him like that, and it was even also upsetting for others close to him. None of us knew how it would all end, and even when Tony saw the danger, it didn't change him. Instead he carried on along his own road to destruction.

Many times in my playing days I had seen how drug use starts. It is often through extreme tiredness or the feeling of being unable to perform the same show you had done a million times already. It becomes too much, where once it was so easy. There follows a strong need to get some form of assistance, some stimulation, anything that can help give a 'lift': and get him or her through the performance – just one more time.

Your show, instead of being a joy, has become an appalling nightmare, and on stage second best will definitely not do. No artist ever wants to become boring. With drugs you can find inspiration, but then you begin to live on borrowed time, that is the price you have to pay. Drink and drugs can only work for a limited period of time. Then it's all downhill.

This was the road that Tony Sheridan was on. But I never discussed it with him. I noticed that Gene Vincent had a terrible problem too. Breakfast on tour was a bottle of Vodka. I saw it happening – I was on tour with Gene in the UK and also in Israel. In the end it was alcohol that played a big part in killing him (Gene died aged 36 in October 1971).

It is unbearable to watch someone destroying themselves,especially when that person is a friend, because that is what Tony Sheridan was to me. But it was difficult, as there was nothing I could do to help him. I believe Tony regretted much of his life: particularly when he arrived in his final years. But they were years filled with activity and well worth living.

His only consolation was in making people happy through music. He told me so. These thoughts came later in life and I read it in his letters: how he struggled to put things right in an unselfish way and through his music (which I shall tell you more about later).

Up until then there was no hint of regret about anything during the 'good' years, when he and I were young and new. But, as I have said, drugs were one of the things we never discussed. It was too painful for both of us. It was a taboo subject, and we left it alone. But I could plainly see the harm it was doing him.

While all this was going through my mind, Tony was lying under a customer's table, close to the stage in the 'Top Ten', supposedly doing a show. It was weird. But who am I to judge? I am not blameless. As I said my problem was alcohol, I drank too much, and alcohol is a drug, too, and could also cause me to lose control.

But we just didn't talk about it, even though I knew criticism between friends can be healthy, provided it avoids being patronizing or destructive. I have always thought it better to be honest and speak my mind than be a coward and say nothing. At the same time I don't ever remember Tony criticizing me, or anyone else, although everyone has something to be ashamed of. He did however offer me advice, but again, never in an offensive way.

Our honesty did serve to bring us closer together, but as I said, drugs was a taboo subject. Tony was, at that time, re-evaluating his own life during this later period, wondering what else he could turn his many talents to.

He wrote to me in one of his letters dated 27.9.71 about following a different career...

"Dear Old Mate, It was great to see you over here, after so long. Pity there wasn't a bit more time to get together. I'll certainly visit you when I'm next in England – maybe we can have another 'blow' together! I've often thought seriously about doing something completely different – something absolutely nutty, like the Army or even the Police or Customs – but every time I'm on that stage, letting off steam, and the crowd's there with me, I'm in my element. It must be in my blood or something. In a way I envy you, but then again a man's gotta be free...Oh yeahh. How's the force treating you constable? Great I hope. How is the wife/ kids? Fine? Great. Write if you have the time, and let me know what's going on in sunny Southampton, I'd appreciate it... Hope you're all well,

God bless... Your old comrade, Tony"

It was always good to hear from him and of course it was inevitable that he continued doing what he loved doing most, (and what he was best at doing.) He was born to be an entertainer. My talent didn't compare with Tony's − although I was a good bass player, and was with him longer than any other British bassist. But I can't even claim the credit for that. It was Tony who had taught me how to play: He was a teacher to the end!

Sadly I knew the break-up of the 'Jets' was coming. How I knew is not clear. But it was without doubt one of the best bands to come out of the London cellar clubs, where it all began, and now the 'Jets' would be no more. Tony and I were the last of the originals still together. He had driven most of the band's replacements away, including Ringo Starr who, joined us after Rory Storm and the 'Hurricanes' broke up while in

Hamburg – leaving Ringo without work.

Now, without contracts, there was nothing tying the 'Jets' to the 'Top Ten' and nothing tying the 'Top Ten' to the 'Jets' which left the club able to decide themselves who they wanted and who they didn't; loyalty didn't come into it. And in the end, Tony was asked to stay while the rest of the band was asked to leave. It was as simple as that. I didn't blame Tony for taking up the offer made to him by the 'Top Ten' club. The life of a musician is a precarious one, you take what you can – while you can. I did rejoin him at the 'Star Club' later.

Bert Kaempfert (Producer at Polydor Records) had seen Tony Sheridan's potential and had used 'the 'Jets', (having first changed their name to the 'Beat Brothers') to record a number of Tony's songs, but as Tony no longer had his own band at the 'Top Ten', Bert Kaempfert had asked The Beatles to back Tony Sheridan at Polydor instead, as both Tony and The Beatles were already playing at the 'Top Ten' together, and working on various projects. It was the beginning of their collaboration and joint recordings.

For Tony, working with The Beatles must have been like starting afresh all over again. He had always felt a need to 'teach' and did so with each new member of his backing band, or whoever he happened to be working with at the time, which included The Beatles. But his teaching was not always as welcome as it was in the days of the London cellar clubs, or earlier at his sixth form Grammar School, when he was the leader of the school orchestra. However, from his later letters, it was clear that Tony Sheridan's close collaboration with The Beatles was to continue long after they left Hamburg.

It was sad to see Tony working so often alone after rejecting Brian Epstein's offer to carry on working with The Beatles in England. But he didn't complain, he always had work. He didn't feel a need for a manager during those early days of rock 'n' roll: but nowadays nearly everyone in show-biz needs someone to represent them. The 'Jets' had been stuck in a rut for a long time and were going nowhere, mainly because we had no manager, and Tony Sheridan didn't want one.

In Germany big shows had passed us by – except for the UK or foreign tours, when backing Gene Vincent, or later when Tony Sheridan and the band 'Beat Brothers were invited to join the Chubby Checker grand European tour, thanks to Don Arden.

Don was was a famous British manager, who saw Tony's talent, but said, when it was suggested that he took Tony on permanently:

'No thanks, I can never find him when I need him' (a phrase that was to haunt Tony).

Tony Sheridan and the 'Jets' should have left Germany long ago – as The Beatles and many other top bands had done, otherwise success wasn't going to happen for us. It wasn't Hamburg that made The Beatles famous, it was their talent: their song-writing, their recordings, but more importantly their tours. It wasn't until they left Germany that great things began to happen for them, and they became world stars and fully recognized for what an awesome talent they were. Tony helped them as he had helped many others, but he couldn't help himself.

Sadly there was no one who knew how to deal with Tony Sheridan: or how to manage him, and most of all, how to bring some discipline and order into his life. Ever since his early days he had been like the shiny metal ball in a pinball machine, careering around in whatever direction it was pushed or pulled. He really was a 'loose cannon' – as he had described himself to me several times, but was also like the 'Candle born to burn unseen'.

Some say Bert Kaempfert was Tony's manager, before The Beatles came to Hamburg, but Mr Kaempfert was never a rock 'n' roll manager. He was a world famous band leader, still writing 'swing' numbers and producing big band sounds, dance, and jazz music, while at the same time, trying to produce rock 'n' roll records for Tony Sheridan! The wide gaps in each others music didn't mix and the partnership wasn't working for them. I was there at some of the recording sessions with Tony's backing band, and saw for myself how little Bert Kaempferts knew of what rock and roll was all about.

But more disastrous for Polydor, was missing out on re-signing The Beatles when Polydor was the first to have them in their recording studios –

at a time when they were Tony Sheridan's backing band, and making joint recordings with him.

Bert Kaempfert later admitted he 'didn't know how to use The Beatles talent', which also explained his problem with Tony Sheridan' at Polydor. Tony Sheridan had minimal guidance from Bert Kaempfert, although, to be honest, in Tony's case it probably wouldn't have made any difference! Tony Sheridan did his own thing, and was a handful for any manager!

It was around this time that the offer was made by Brian Epstein, inviting Tony to return with The Beatles to the UK and to continue working with them. It was an offer which Tony told me about in a letter explaining what he was doing between 1960-62...

"I made my first solo recordings with The Beatles as my backing group produced by Bert Kaempfert. Then, four months of intensive work

with The Beatles in Hamburg. Joint recordings with The Beatles as my backing group produced by Bert Kaempfert attracted the attention of manager Brian Epstein. An offer to return with them to England was resisted (with no regrets)."

Why Tony Sheridan had 'resisted the offer' from Brian Epstein to return to England with The Beatles, and to do so 'with no regrets' is a mystery to me and everyone else.

It was only after researching information for this book and re-reading Tony's letters, that I discovered information, which throws more light on the importance of Tony Sheridan's involvement with The Beatles during their early development, and how highly he was regarded by them. Tony also worked with Gerry Marsden, who Tony says stole, 'You'll never walk alone' from Tony's repertoire!

When Tony Sheridan is talked about now, it is

mainly because of his association with The Beatles, and his music collaboration with them in Hamburg. But, according to Tony (in his letters) it was much more extensive than that and continued for much longer in the UK and long after The Beatles were famous. This makes it easier to understand why they called him 'Teacher'. But it had still been a puzzling choice not to return to the UK with them.

With The Beatles backing him at Polydor, Tony had recorded, 'My Bonnie' before The Beatles left Germany for England without him. 'My Bonnie' eventually sold over a million copies, and Tony was later awarded a Gold Album by the music industry, the first formal music recognition he had received. 'My Bonnie' was a song he had sung many times before and it was Polydor who had suggested he recorded it, having realised there was a huge market for this Scottish folk song, which was well known to many children learning English at schools in Europe, America and many other parts of the world.

Having rejected the chance to join The Beatles Tony was on his own again and there was no point in me talking to him any more about the future. He had already chosen the path he wanted to follow and it would always be in the same unchanging way, with no plans which would restrain him. It was a simple one – just keep going. If I had questioned it, he would only have said what he had said before: about being Tony Sheridan, the 'loose cannon'.

The bottom line for the 'Jets was that we were grateful to have been in London and then Germany at the beginning of that incredible rock and roll period. It is something none of us shall ever forget. We had a lot of fun playing in Hamburg and saw the joy on the young German fans faces on hearing us play. They were awesome times and despite the many disappointments and problems we would simply solve the ones we could, and ignore the ones we couldn't and then move on. Something every rock and roll band must do.

That's not the way to end it all as Tony and I (together with new band members), were to have a great many more music adventures which I shall also tell you about in this story. They are all great memories that nobody can take away from us, nor from the many fans who are now much older, but still remember the momentous 60's, and are still glad to talk about the days when the 'Englander' first played in Hamburg.

As I said earlier The Beatles had left Hamburg and gone on to greater things, leaving Tony Sheridan behind, having learnt much from him.

They were grateful for what Tony had taught them, and they have repeatedly said so over the years.

We had all learnt from each other and The Beatles don't owe Tony anything. He had given his talents freely, as he had done to me, and to all those who had crossed his path, including some who didn't appreciate his teaching methods! But most of all he had helped that scruffy, mediocre band of the 'Indra' days, later to be called The Beatles, to make progress.

I stayed with Tony as long as I could, and only wished I had met him long before, so that he could become my teacher, too – I had already learnt much from him and wanted to learn more. But we sometimes need to move on to other things, and leave our regrets behind.

Tony Sheridan made a difference to all of us as a teacher, including The Beatles. It is something no honest member of the band will ever forget. Yes, Tony was a tyrant, but many teachers of any worth are tyrants too! The end will sometimes justify the means!

What really matters is the door to Germany had been opened for the introduction of many British bands to their German fans. We brought our own distinctive rock and roll, 'sound' with us, which we developed from the Americans and changed, to suit ourselves.

British rock and roll bands have spread out, not only to Europe but to all the continents of the world, and then back to America again via The Beatles and many other great British bands. Today many other countries have great bands too.

But let's go back to the earlier story about our leaving the 'Top Ten'. I distinctly remember sensing some manoeuvrings going on, a kind of nervous foreboding in the club. It was as if something was about to happen, it was the same feeling I had experienced before: when we were forced to leave the 'Kaiser Keller' and 'bad vibes' were in the air.

This time it started with a decline in customer numbers visiting the 'Top Ten' and then other people, who we had never met, were getting heavily involved in the organisation and management of the club, whereas Peter Eckhorn, the owner and his family, were less visible, or involved in the important decision-makings. The 'Top Ten' was losing its way.

The constant state of disarray and the feeling of insecurity was not helped by Tony's insistence on perfection from all of us in the band. The high standards he demanded were targeted at everyone except himself. His problem was his own behaviour and lack of tactful man-management, which affected the band badly; especially among the newer members.

There are few musicians who like being told what to play, and how to play it, as I have already mentioned. Especially when much of Tony's 'teaching' was not done in private, as it should be, but on stage during a show and in front of the audience. It was this that resulted in many of his musicians leaving the band and moving on. The 'Jets' had been going through the motions without any plan for the future. We were stumbling around not knowing what tomorrow may bring – whereas our future success had looked bright when we first began to make records with Tony Sheridan at Polydor.

In the end, as I have already said, Tony and I were the only ones left of the original 'Jets', that had left London in June 1960. And if you look at the story of Tony Sheridan's life, you will see how often he ended up on his own: as a solo act. That's how it was when he was younger, and that's how it was in later life. And now all of us, except Tony, were given notice to quit the 'Top Ten', leaving Tony Sheridan on his own again, sitting in with visiting bands, and working closely with The Beatles, or playing as a solo artist'.

It was there at the 'Top Ten that Tony's more serious collaboration with The Beatles first began, leading to the offer by Brian Epstein for Tony to continue working with them in England.

For Tony and me it seemed to be the end of an era and separation, and I didn't expect to see him again. I had made other plans for the future, and a big part of it was to marry my German bride-to-be, Ingrid, and start a new life in England with a 'proper' job. But Tony and I agreed we would always stay touch, and we did, right up to the end of his life in 2013.

Before Tony and I finally said goodbye, there was a visit to Hamburg by an American aircraft carrier, the USS 'Nimitz' and the majority of the customers at the 'Top Ten' that night were made up almost exclusively of US sailors (about 600 or more).

At first all was peaceful: they loved Tony Sheridan, and sang along with him, at the same time drinking heavily. I don't think they were expecting him to be so good. Before long a continuous flow of drinks were arriving on stage for all of us in the band.

Unlike the British Royal Navy, alcohol was not allowed on US fighting ships and, of course, when the US sailors got to port, they tried to make up for it by drinking as much as possible, and getting off their heads on strong drink. It wasn't long before what started as a minor scuffle became a full-scale riot between the sailors and the club bouncers. Very soon every waiter and even the bar-staff joined in to quell what was now a serious disorder.

We stopped playing to watch the show as chairs, bottles, and ash-trays whistled past our heads, similar to what happened when we played at the 'Kaiser Keller'. But this was worse as the crew of the 'Nimitz', was much bigger. It was the best fight I had ever seen.

Tony was tempted to join in – I could tell by his wide excited eyes and twitchy body language. But I was glad he didn't. This was a serious one, and if he did decide to get involved, he would surely get hurt. There followed a hundred or so smaller individual fights, with German against sailor, and sailor against anyone German, including the customers.

At times there were groups of twenty sailors

fighting the same number of waiters and doormen. Then more bouncers came pouring in from different clubs along the Reeperbahn. Tony stood up, getting ever more excited; Then sat down again, I was worried about him and stayed close – ready to drag him away before he could pile in and join the fight.

The Germans, as always, were well organised, and soon the whole dance-floor and hidden alcoves were a mass of struggling bodies. While in every corner, men were frantically fighting their own private battles, one to one. Meanwhile still more club staff came rushing in, carrying their favourite weapons: clubs, whips, coshes and knuckledusters.

The fight was going nowhere. Finally there was a stand-off between the two sides.

The US sailors stayed at one end of the club and the German waiters and bouncers at the other.

A truce was negotiated and each of the two groups was asked to put forward a single man to represent them. It was agreed that whoever won would settle the whole fight for his side, once and for all. One US sailor was to fight one German representative of the club staff and both sides would accept the winner and end the fighting.

The US sailors got together and talked quietly about who it was to be, and eventually put forward a tall young sailor in his twenties, who looked like he could handle himself.

The 'Top Ten' side put forward the club manager. He was another big man with a fearsome reputation. The flag was dropped and the two men began to fight – backwards and forwards it went until the US sailor was finally beaten and peace magically returned to the club once more. Everyone sat down and continued drinking, but a tense unstable calm lingered over the club, and at times it looked as if the slightest thing would start the ball rolling again.

But in time everyone slowly relaxed, the fight was over. The decision as to who had won was accepted, and the American sailors were sitting down on whatever chairs were still available and unbroken, and continued with their drinking, surrounded by damaged tables, and pieces of wood used as clubs. Also lying around or propped up against the walls were the bodies of injured sailors and waiters waiting for an ambulance. And still the police had not intervened.

I had seen many fights in my time at sea, especially when we visited French Canada, and similar things happened at the big night clubs in Montreal and Quebec. These, too, could end in stalemate, and we all simply moved on to the next club. But this fight in Hamburg was as I said, the biggest and best I had ever seen, and our band had a great view of it all from our position on the stage. I was with Tony again when trouble started in a Reeperbahn bar. This time it was during a visit by Royal Navy sailors from a British destroyer.

The Brits, too, had plenty to drink and began getting into arguments with the waiters.

It got out of hand when the 'Brits' started calling the Germans, 'Nazis', and soon another full-blown fight broke out between the Royal Navy and the bouncers, which spilled out onto the Reeperbahn. The 'Brits' were given a good hiding, mistakenly thinking the Germans would fight 'fair', using only their fists, but they didn't. They used every weapon they could lay their hands on. Fights seemed to follow Tony Sheridan wherever he went!

After a spell doing various labouring jobs in

Hamburg, I was invited to return to music again, first with the 'All Round Men', a German band managed by Manfred Woitalla, (later owner of the 'Star Palast' in Lueneburg) and then with the 'Bats', managed by Juergen Dankers. Both were very good bands.

Then I received a letter from Tony asking me to join him in a new band (the 'Star Combo') which was to become the resident band at the newly-opened 'Star Club' in Hamburg. I joined him as soon as I could. Tony now had a complete band once more. But deep down I believe he preferred to express his talent on his own, whenever that was possible. He had no need of huge audiences, or even a regular band .– smaller audiences were much more personal, with fewer things to go wrong, and he was also in complete charge. But whenever rock 'n' roll was played, as at the 'Star

Club', he would need at least a three piece band.

Much later (1975/77) he wrote to me about a phase he was going through, and telling me of his solo recordings and TV appearances in Hamburg and Landskrona (Sweden) with the accent on acoustic music. It confirmed his preference to play as a solo artist, and towards the end of his playing days, he did play much more on his own. It could explain the illogical decisions Tony had made and why he had rejected great opportunities to secure his future in the rock 'n roll world. He was now moving towards both blues music and the classics.

This was, in my view why he turned down the offer made by Brian Epstein to return to England with The Beatles, and why he had sabotaged a career in British Television in the early 60's after being invited to play in the BBC TV rock 'n roll shows. Why else did he turn down the chance to go to America with Joey Dee and the Starliters?

Could it be he had no intention of continuing with rock 'n roll? I put the idea forward only as an explanation for Tony's actions which at first glance seemed to be an artist, wishing only to press the self-destruct button. But Tony was an intelligent guy: he must have realized the outcome of what he was doing. He did things his own way – not caring about fame, fortune and missed chances. For him, the only way to keep both control and independence, was to play alone: to shun all ambition that didn't suit him, and do everything his own way.

When we left London for Hamburg, Tony was just one of the 'Jets'. But in Hamburg everything changed. Tony was now solely in charge and none of us saw it coming.

That was exactly what he wanted: To have control and do things his own way, which he couldn't have done if he had stayed with The

Beatles. But because of his obvious talent the band had allowed him to take charge, and do it without interference. But now, instead of a fixed and planned direction there was only a vacuum. We were a ship without a rudder.

Tony's inward-looking nature: having no ambitions for the future, and with no manager in place to plan our direction, and no sign of things ever changing for the better, meant the downfall of the 'Jets' – chaos means there is nothing to focus on, or tell us where we were going – nor did anyone appear on the horizon to give us hope: which all successful bands needed – including The Beatles.

The great bands always found a manager, one who was also a leader: someone who knew where he was going, but this was not for Tony. He saw no great need for it, although he must have known it was impossible to make things happen without someone working on it.

To Tony, all this organised stuff was irrelevant, and as long as we all played what he wanted us to play, and he was able to carry on as he had always done, he was happy.

It didn't matter whether the band liked it or not! He would play without us if necessary, as he demonstrated once at the 'Star Club', when the band (now the 'Star Combo'), walked off stage after a dispute, leaving Tony and Roy Young to carry on playing alone, which Tony did very well. Roy was unsure whether to join us or not, and was worried about his contract.

If you didn't like criticism from Tony, or you took offence at being told off in front of an audience. Tough! That's how it was: Take it or leave it. But despite the many problems, the standard of music in the band was always high.

The downside to Tony's one man show was that we often had a vacancy for a replacement band member, and it was often a drummer.

Few drummers wanted to stay and be abused by Tony Sheridan, and as already mentioned earlier, our singer/drummer from the original 'Jets' (Jimmy Ward), had by then already left us, as did several drummers after him.

One of them was a black American named, Alvin, who played alongside Buddy Rich, the world famous Jazz drummer. Buddy Rich was also a singer, and when singing, he needed a drummer to back him: this is where Alvin came in.

Alvin had left Buddy Rich while on a European jazz tour to Scandinavia and hoped to stay on in Germany. He came looking for work at the 'Top Ten'.

We tried him out but he was one of the many

jazz-orientated drummers who, although technically brilliant, couldn't keep a rock beat going without straying off into a jazz riff. We had to turn him down. It wasn't for us.

We also had Tony Cavanaugh, another black American drummer from Indianapolis, then living in Germany. He stayed with us for quite a while. He, too, was a good drummer and an even better singer. Then, while still at the 'Top Ten', we had a German drummer named Ingo Thomas, who was technically very good and a nice guy, but he didn't have a 'feel' for rock   music and also eventually left us, with Tony helping him on his way.

Ingo had shared the accommodation at the club with us, and most of us weren't sorry when he had gone, as every day he brought anti-social food with him in his lunch box, and, much to our disgust, insisted on eating it upstairs in the accommodation, and stinking the place out. His favourite food was German 'Hartzer' cheese (one of the most unlikeliest cheeses ever to be called 'food'!). Even the busiest public toilets in London's Piccadilly couldn't smell worse than 'Hartzer' I can smell it now as I write, ugh!

There were other drummers who joined our band, including Jimmy Doyle, an Irish boy from Dublin and a wonderfully gifted drummer; He played with us in Hamburg and in Frankfurt, before the band was finally no more.

The 'Arcadia' Club in Frankfurt was intended to be my last 'gig' before I left Germany and return to England. It was while on stage playing there, that we heard the terrible news that President Kennedy had been shot. The Beatles were playing at the 'Star Club' in Hamburg at the same time as we played at the 'Arcadia; They also made a special appearance at the 'Kaiser Keller' where they had once played.

Interestingly, apart from drummers, there were also other musicians looking for work at the 'Top Ten' while we were there. All had been attracted by the 'new' music. One of them was an incredible Gypsy guitarist, Elek Bacisk, related to the great guitarist Django Reinhart. Tony and I, as well as everyone else present that evening in the 'Top Ten', were completely mesmerized by his emotive and technically brilliant mastery of the guitar. Sadly there was no place for him in our band. His music, although beautiful, was alien to us, as I'm sure ours was to him, and there was unfortunately no way we could have played together.

The last drummer to leave us when we played at the 'Top Ten' was Ringo Starr, who first joined us from a Liverpool band, 'Rory Storm and the Hurricanes', which had broken up in Hamburg around the time the 'Jets were playing at the 'Top Ten' club.

Ringo was looking for work at that time, and was not ready to return home to Liverpool. He joined us for a trial, we saw how his simple drum-style fitted in well with what Tony Sheridan wanted, and more importantly, Ringo was keen to learn. Tony, true to his nature, was willing to teach him as to what was required.

In my view Ringo already had all the most important qualities that many other drummers don't have: he could keep the beat like clockwork, he didn't speed up, he didn't 'drag' and he didn't change the drum rhythm halfway through the number, as many more technically gifted drummers were inclined to do. The great blues singer, BB King later said of Ringo, after they had played together, 'Ringo's playing is like a clock, Tick-tock, tick-tock'.

Ringo was the best drummer we had, until the great Johnny Watson came along and joined the 'Star Combo' at the newly-opened 'Star Club'. Meanwhile at the 'Top Ten', Tony did as Tony does: and knowingly or unknowingly, drove Ringo away.

He had only been with us at the 'Top Ten' for a short time before Tony turned on him, in the same way he had turned on all the other drummers who had ever played for us.

'What the fuck are you playing Ringo?' (Ringo had just started getting to grips with the drum part for Ray Charles', 'What'd I say'), which was a bit different from the usual rock 'n' roll rhythms – Ringo stopped playing and looked nonchalantly up. He was an easy-going, unflappable scouser. Tony took off his guitar in front of the audience and went over to him,

'Get off the drums!' which Ringo did. Then

Tony, the noisiest and worst drummer I have ever heard, attempted to show Ringo what rhythm he should have been playing. It was humiliating to watch, and understandably few drummers were prepared to take it.

My own method of dealing with Tony was to completely ignore him, or give back as good as I got. A couple of months later Ringo left us and went back to Liverpool. He wasn't prepared to stick it out either, and I don't blame him.

I heard later, not long after he arrived home in Liverpool, and after playing at a Butlins holiday camp, he had joined The Beatles. I didn't agree with Tony's method of teaching, but I cannot deny that it worked. But Tony must have known the effect it had on his fellow musicians, and why so many had left him, but he was uncompromising in everything he did.

But if you were taught anything at all by Tony

Sheridan, it stayed with you for the rest of your life, and was sure to make you a better musician: as it did with every member of Tony's current and previous bands as well as for The Beatles. It was no different for Ringo.

When he left us he was greatly improved, and the best drummer we had taken on so far.

Ringo had come from being the 'dragging' drummer of his early 'Hurricanes' days, to one who could keep the beat like a drum-machine. He was also a quick learner: able to do all that was asked of him, and even before joining The Beatles, I was told Ringo was in demand by other bands in Liverpool. The drummer who followed Ringo, when the 'Star Combo' was resident band at the 'Star Club" was the great Johnny Watson. Johnny had arrived at the 'Star Club' with 'Tex Roberg and the Graduates' from Southampton, and he was the only drummer we had who was better than Ringo Starr.

We already had a stand-in drummer soon after Ringo had left us, but Tony was far from happy with him, and 'stole' the great Johnny Watson from the 'Graduates' by making Johnny an offer he couldn't refuse, (more money!) and also doing a swap (their drummer for ours).

Johnny was a Southampton boy whose family originally came from Liverpool. As a novice musician he began by first playing lead guitar, and then drums, which he took to like a hawk to flying – he was a natural. His lead-guitar experience helped him work out what was needed from the drums before Tony Sheridan had time to tell Johnny what to play!

Tex and the 'Graduates' were not happy that Tony Sheridan had spirited Johnny away.

But that's how things were in those days; There

156

were no contracts within the bands!

Johnny was later offered the chance to join The Beatles: who saw how good he was, but he turned it down to stay with the 'Star Combo'. We were glad he did, and he later told me he never regretted it. Money isn't everything! He was happy with us and we sounded great together! To us, Johnny's talent as a drummer (compared to all other drummers) was the difference between a Jaguar motor car and a Ford.

Much later Johnny told me about visiting the now famous Beatles when they were on tour, playing at the 'Gaumont' in his home town of Southampton. As soon as Ringo saw Johnny backstage, he went down on his knees: bowing and scraping as if in worship.

We all felt the same way about Johnny Watson – he was a fabulous drummer and we couldn't have found a better one anywhere. Drummers like him are like rocking horse droppings – you just don't see many about!

As resident band at the 'Star Club' the 'Star Combo' was expected to back any artists arriving from America, or elsewhere who, for whatever reason, didn't have a band with them. As a result, we backed Tommy Rowe and Brenda Lee, and also played alongside the many other great American stars who appeared at the 'Star Club',while, Roy Young and Tony Sheridan continued to perform their own individual 'sets' – as stars in their own right.

Roy Young was already well known as a rock and roll legend, having played alongside the greats. Roy told me how Little Richard had said to him, while both were playing at the 'Star Club, 'Roy,You sound just like me!' Roy had also recorded with Chuck Berry, David Bowie, and later with The Beatles, as well as working with many others, including Cliff Bennett and the great, David Bedford, whose many-faceted talents encompassed: classical, music hall, and later rock music.

Having the 'Star Combo' backing them in those exhilarating days, allowed all the great visiting American stars to shine, while inspiring Tony Sheridan, Roy Young, Johnny Watson, Ricky Barnes, and myself to play the best music we had ever played. The 'Star Combo' was later recorded 'live' on an LP, 'Twist at the Star Club', by Philips records. They were heady and happy times: when rock 'n' roll was still new, and every visiting star was different.

There was an abiding feeling of freedom in the mainly German audience; freedom for the young to reject everything that went before. They were no longer willing to hide their now rebellious spirit, and it was soon evident, this new-found freedom wasn't going to go away. It is still with us today, as more and more German rock bands are springing up.

The 60's wasn't a good time to be a parent; German teenagers, as in England, didn't listen to their elders so much, and it was hard being a mum or dad. But it was an incredible experience to be a part of all that, and at the same time to be playing in a great band.

Johnny Watson made playing the drums look incredibly easy; Tony Crombie, the great drummer, band-leader, and producer, (Johnny's teacher), had taught him well.

But Tony Sheridan was in for a shock; Johnny was someone not used to being intimidated or humiliated; despite being of small build and looking much younger than he was; Johnny had his own way of dealing with Tony Sheridan, and it was a more subtle method than mine.

Whenever Tony was being aggressive, rude, or unreasonable to him, Johnny would say nothing, and wait for Tony to sing a suitable number, usually a wild up-tempo rock song, and when it was at its height, Johnny would suddenly add a short, crippling, change of beat, lasting just a split second, which somehow, (and I still don't know how), confused Tony so much that it completely disrupted his timing and sabotaged the song, causing him to stop.

Tony looked round at us in anger, having no idea what had happened to the great number he was singing just moments ago, and which, up until now, was going so well. I tried not to smile, or do anything to give the game away.

But I knew who had caused the disruption – although I had no idea how Johnny had done it. I saw The Beatles smile from their usual seats in the front row, where they often sat when Tony sang and played: carefully watching his every move. But I'm not sure if they had spotted what had happened. Tony was still staring at Johnny, who was by now wearing his famous 'innocent' look, and although Tony suspected it was the drums that had caused the hiccup, he wasn't sure – by then we were all playing perfectly in time again, waiting for Tony to continue. After the number had ended Tony looked over at Johnny,

'What happened there, Johnny?' who just shrugged his shoulders,

'No idea, mate' I loved him, and now Tony, too, was forced to respect Johnny a bit more.

I will never forget that 'innocent' look and Johnny's clever way of getting his own back and bringing Tony down – thereby helping to make up for what Tony had so often done to humiliate other musicians – but now he knew how it felt being on the receiving end.

Johnny died in 2013, in Perth, Western Australia. It was in the same year that Tony passed away. Johnny and I were regularly in touch, right up until his death, and Johnny was due to visit England from Australia and stay with Ingrid and I – he didn't make it. He had received his 'tap on the shoulder': It was time to go. He had done his bit.

Going back to Ringo, I remember him as a good guy – never flashy; He and I hit it off from the first day he joined our band, and we shared a room in the upstairs accommodation at the 'Top Ten'. He was an uncomplicated person, although his conversations were a bit dry, and even sardonic, so that sometimes it was hard to tell if he was joking or being serious – It   was just the secretive side of Ringo: He could always hide his feelings well.

At that time when we were together, his main talking point, apart from music, was his old humped-back 'Standard Vanguard', a car which he once owned, and which was still close to his heart. I casually asked him why he was called 'Ringo'. He simply held out his hand to show me the many rings on his fingers, which made it obvious, but to be honest, I hadn't noticed them before!

Despite not looking much like a film star, Ringo was very popular with the German girls. They liked him because he was genuine – what you see is what you get. I remember the girlfriend he was with at the time he and I were together; a blond girl, really beautiful. Also noticeable was that, unlike John and Paul, Ringo never showed off, and was always respectful to others, which together with his shyness and good manners, attracted the girls to him. After playing, he and I would go out to get something to eat, which usually meant soup or a hamburger in the nearby 'Grosser Freiheit'.

One evening, on our way out to eat once more, Hamburg was hit by a power cut, which blacked out most of the city. The Reeperbahn lost its lights, the restaurants closed, and the clubs and strip joints could no longer do business. The trams stopped too; In fact everything stopped except the taxis. Nothing could function without power, and people were now realizing it, and rushing around in confusion.

For the German people it must have been like the war years were back again. Ringo and I were lost, and wandered about in the dark, unable to recognize anything.

'Any idea where we can we get something to

eat, Col?' asked Ringo, quietly. We were both hungry. In the darkness I could just about see crowds of agitated people joining queues. What they were queueing for, I don't know; It may have been instinctive.

In times of trouble: when people see a queue they join it. But it still didn't look good.

'Just a minute Ringo', I left him to find a phone and make a call and then rushed back,

'Its all fixed, we're going to Ingrid's house. We got into one of the many taxi's, which had raced into Hamburg to cope with the huge surge of unexpected business, and set off for Ingrid's house on the outskirts of Hamburg.

Ringo was made really welcome by Ingrid's family, as they had done with me, when I first met them. Ringo was quieter than usual, and quite shy. But the family put him at ease, as I knew they would. Food was prepared for us: boiled eggs, cooked on an old wood-fired log stove, and served with German bread. It wasn't much, but it was better than nothing.

Ringo didn't speak much German at that time, nor did Ingrid or her parents speak any English, but I was able to interpret for all of us (thanks to a friendly on-going competition between Tony Sheridan and me as to who spoke the best German!).

Ingrid's mum and dad got on well with Ringo and fussed around him as if he were royalty. Ringo obviously liked both of them, especially her dad, who was a really nice guy.

He had worked for the railway as a train driver during the war. One day his train got badly shot-up by low-flying spitfires, and he had some terrible scars on his back to show for it. The Russian prisoner, forced to work with him as a fireman, was killed.

He also told me how he and his wife risked their lives during those awful times, by taking a Jewish woman into their home and giving her food. She was one of a party of women from a nearby work-camp, who had been digging the roads in the middle of a cold winter.

Ingrid's parents offered the woman some winter clothes, too, but the Jewish lady refused, as it would have put Ingrid's family in danger, as well as herself. The guards would know the clothes were not hers. Not all Germans were bad people when it came to the Jews.

On another occasion Ingrid's father was arrested and taken into Hamburg for refusing to put the swastika flag up on his house, as he should have done each morning (all owners of houses in that area were required to do so by the police). He was taken into the centre of Hamburg to a school playground and required to march around all day singing patriotic songs: at the end of the day he was given a severe warning and taken home again.

Tony wasn't with Ringo and me in the evening of the blackout – in fact I rarely saw him during the evenings at all; he was spending more and more time with others who lived on the wild side of Hamburg's night life. He also had a new girlfriend; I always left him to it.

After finishing our food, we thanked Ingrid's parents for their kindness and walked all the way back to the 'Top Ten' in St Pauli as there were no more taxis available. Next day everything was back to normal and power was restored; You can't keep the Germans down for long!

Ringo told me more about 'Rory Storm and the 'Hurricanes': The band Ringo had been a part of when they played at the 'Kaiser Keller', and which later broke up (for reasons I didn't ask about). I had seen Rory Storm around and he was often alone. I would talk to him and he told me he wanted to stay in Hamburg, but he didn't have any work.

It was around the time Ringo joined us in the 'Jets',and we played at the 'Top Ten'. None of the English band's jobs were safe in Hamburg around this time, as more and more bands began to arrive, giving the club owners more choice and now, as Rory found out, it was becoming more and more difficult to find work.

Unfortunately, the first thing you noticed, when talking to Rory was his terrible stutter. It wasn't just the occasional word, but a whole series of words. Anyone who didn't know him wouldn't believe he was a rock and roll singer. How could he have such a bad stutter and still be a singer? But he really was a singer, and a good one too!

His main difficulty was his normal day to day conversations away from the stage. Then, as he spoke, his head would shake violently, as if trying to force the words out.

But it was strange how Rory never stuttered when he sang on stage. I saw it for myself when he later sang with us at the 'Flurschaenke', where we later played, on leaving the 'Top Ten', and where Tony Sheridan was to joined us. The Beatles had by then gone back to the UK without Tony. I liked Rory a lot, and occasionally, together with Ringo, the three of us we would go around together, looking at the many erotic and fascinating, Reeperbahn shops. Rory still hadn't found work at that time (after leaving the 'Kaiser Keller') and Ringo had been playing with us at the 'Top Ten'. It seemed everything that was illegal in England could be bought on the Reeperbahn: guns of all makes and shapes, knuckledusters and no end of other weapons.

But also for sale were the hilarious 'kinky' materials and objects used in the many houses of 'ill repute' situated along the whole length of this notorious highway. If you couldn't find what you were looking for anywhere else, you were almost certain to find it in the shops on the Reeperbahn! My lasting memory of Rory Storm is when, together with Ringo, we went to the low-price Woolworth store, on the main part of the Reeperbahn. Rory needed some laces for his trainers and was down on his luck, and short of money.

I still have a picture of him in my mind of him haggling with a confused young checkout girl over the price of some shoelaces, his blond hair shaking wildly as he stuttered out his message. The shop assistant looked at me, smiling, not quite sure what was going on, and thinking he was pretending – and didn't really stutter at all. Rory kept asking how much the cheap shoelaces were: and then tried to negotiate a lower price for them.

'They are twenty pfennigs' said the shop-girl, searching our faces for a clue about Rory's intentions and why he was acting so strangely. She kept looking at us, with a pained and puzzled look, clearly seeking help. What could I say? I would have gladly given Rory the amount she asked for, but Rory stopped me, indicating I should put my money away – he was only having fun with the assistant. But the situation wasn't funny any more.

'Nein!' she said firmly – realizing at last that Rory was teasing her. Rory then stopped doing it and paid the full amount. These are the kinds of things you never forget, and although it was funny at the time, it wasn't really something to laugh about. In a way it was quite a pathetic thing to do.

But I suppose we all do stupid things sometimes.

But all credit to Rory; He had overcome much in his life, and achieved a lot more than others who had no disabilities. Despite his stutter, he had become a successful singer, and nothing seemed to faze him. He was a wonderful character and I admired his courage greatly. It was sad to hear how he died – following a tragedy at home, leaving him to face something terrible which he was unable to face or overcome.

4. 'FLURSCHAENKE'

It's amazing how we came to be in the 'Flurschaenke'. Having lost the job at the 'Top Ten' we were all, except Tony Sheridan, unemployed. But as one door closes another opens. It was while at the bar in the 'Top Ten', talking to a German friend, Heinzi, that he mentioned a club called the 'Flurschaenke' on the outskirts of Hamburg, where he lived. He suggested we could play there, and offered to introduce me to the owner, an old lady, to see if

175

she would like to change her boring, um' pa' pa' band and bring in an up-to-date 'rock and roll' band like ours.

As soon as Heinzi had said the club was owned by an 'an old lady', I straight away thought it would be a waste of time even going there. Most older people in those early days didn't like rock 'n roll, it was the same in England, but I thought I'd give it a go anyway.

We drove to Lurup, a pleasant residential area of Hamburg, with pretty houses and neat gardens. But it was definitely not 'rock 'n roll' country! It was early evening when walked in. It was not as big as the 'Top Ten', where we last played, but it was big enough for us. It served as the local 'hop' for the teenagers living in this part of town. But they were bored.

On one side of the spacious dance floor was a typical German um' pa' pa' band, as Heinzi said would be there. They were older gentlemen and all dressed up in dark jackets, bow ties, and tails. It looked like a set from an old Hollywood movie.

They were a tired-looking bunch, and looked slowly up as we walked in, their weary eyes following us as we walked over to the bar. It was as if they knew what was coming and their jobs were no longer safe. Heinzi asked to see the owner, and an old lady came out to speak to us. Heinzi spoke quietly to her and told her why we were there. But as soon as he mentioned the idea of English rock-band playing there she didn't seem at all ready (or willing) to up-date, or change, her existing band, even though most of her customers were young people, and this was the nearest place they could meet at weekends. It was a really nice venue, everything clean, ordered and in its place. Typically German.

Heinzi turned on the charm and told the old

lady she must move on if she wanted to survive, times were changing. The old lady wavered a bit – she wasn't earning much from the few regulars who came in, and needed more customers. Heinzi's idea was a good one,

But she was still clearly concerned about the neighbours in the houses nearby.

'What kind of music do you play?' she asked, with a more-than-worried look on her face.

'It's only rock 'n roll' I said, hoping she wouldn't know what rock 'n roll was. But she did, 'nein, nein, nein! die nachbarn' (no! no! no! the neighbours) she said,and pointed to the peaceful-looking houses nearby: clearly worried about the effect our band would have on the people living nearby.

'Wir koennen leise spielen' I told her in my best German (we can play quietly) but I was not being totally honest with her – knowing that rock 'n roll cannot be played quietly, but I liked this place, and wanted to give her a good reason for taking us on.

At last she relented, and against her better judgement, agreed to employ us, starting the following week. The deal included great accommodation which was free and good pay.

I thanked Heinzi as we walked out, but couldn't help noticing the worried looks on the faces of the um' pa' pa' band as we passed them by. But times really were a-changing.

Heinzi drove me back to the 'Top Ten', where I found Tony. He wasn't doing much at that time and The Beatles had gone home to Liverpool. I told him about the 'Flurschaenke' and Tony was immediately up for it. The rest of the band, including our most recent 'Jets' drummer, Tony Cavanaugh, were also up for it too. We started on the following Saturday.

In Lurup the word had already got around that an English band was to play at the local 'hop', and soon the youngsters came streaming in from all over Lurup. The place was packed from the very first evening. Tony loved it there, it was then that it dawned on me he preferred to play in smaller halls and clubs, and had no great yearning for huge audiences and great halls. For him, fame and fortune are not controllable when things are too big.

But there was trouble from the very first night: which lasted right up until we were asked to leave. The problem was that Tony couldn't bring himself to turn down the volume of his amp: no matter how often he was asked to do so, and his wild unshackled guitar-playing could be heard blasting out undiluted rock music half a mile away, to the fury of the neighbours.

Things were turning ugly and the police were called in to quell the noise, but it didn't help and Tony carried on as before. I tried talking to him myself; but that had no effect either. He did everything his own way, and no one could get him to do otherwise.

The old lady owner tried threats, where persuasion had failed. Then the bar manager, who was a bit of a bruiser, waded in and angrily told us to turn the noise down, but that didn't help either. Tony knew only one way to play, and it was loudly and fiercely.

Of course promises were made to the complaining residents, that the sound would be turned down, and sure enough Tony did sometimes start quietly, but was soon letting loose again – having only been quiet for a couple of minutes.

He must have known that it would only be a

matter of time before we were thrown out; But Tony lived on the edge – always choosing the wild side of life, and sod everyone else. In the meantime the many new customers were bringing in much needed financial help, and things were looking up for the club-owner, but the situation couldn't continue as it was.

Some of the bands from Hamburg would come and watch us play, including the out-of-work Rory Storm, mentioned earlier, whose band had broken up and whose drummer (Ringo Starr) had played with us at the 'Top Ten'. Rory would come up on stage and sing a couple of numbers with us at the 'Flurschaenke.' The audience loved him with his shock of blond hair, and attractive off-stage stutter. He sang some great ballads and blues numbers.

He wanted to stay and sing regularly with us, and we would like to have taken him on – but the band already had several singers; Tony Sheridan, Tony Cavanaugh and myself.

It was sad to see Rory so lonely there in Hamburg, but I did help him out whenever I could. It is something we did for all out of work musicians and had done so from our early London cellar-club days, when money was tight (I'm still owed borrowed money!).

It was there at the 'Flurschaenke' that I first met Ingrid, the girl I was to marry. She was there every weekend with a group of her friends. What first attracted me to her, apart from her beautiful smile, was her dancing. She was a great rock and jive dancer, as many of the girls in Hamburg were.

I wasn't very good at approaching girls for the first time and once again left it a bit late. I suppose it was the fear of rejection. But during the break, Tony and me, and some other members of the band, were sitting at a table close to the stage as we usually did.

There were always those others who wanted to be seen with the band and would come and join us. On this particular evening a ski instructor had invited himself to our table. He was a smooth operator, and scanned the dance floor for a likely girl for the evening.

'She's nice!' he said to me, pointing to Ingrid on the other side of the dance floor, and tried to attract her attention. That was enough for me, I decided to be a bit bolder and marched over to her as she talked to a group of her friends. She didn't speak any English other than 'pig' and 'dog' (which, thankfully she didn't direct at me!) and I asked her in my best German if she would like to go out with me to the cinema.

She just smiled,

'I will have to ask my mother first.' she said.

Her group of friends were giggling nearby, but Ingrid was only seventeen, and asking permission of the parents was the way things were done in those innocent days. At first her mother was not happy about me,

'Couldn't you find a nice German boy?' she asked. But she didn't stand in Ingrid's way, and I was eventually accepted into her lovely family.

I never saw the ski-instructor again and Antje, my previous girlfriend, came to the 'Flurschaenke' and gave Ingrid the photo of myself; The same one I had given to Antje when I first met her. It seemed that passing my photo on to Ingrid was a a sign that Antje and I were finished. Ingrid and I have been together ever since. We live in England now and her English is excellent – much more advanced than her 'pig' and 'dog'! She says she learnt English mainly by listening to BBC radio. Tony Sheridan's girl Rosie got on well with

Ingrid, and everyone got on well with Rosie.

Not all German youngsters find learning English easy. I remember being in Travemuende for a 'gig' with Tony. We were sitting on a beautiful sandy beach overlooking the Baltic. Just then a young boy came running past us shouting, 'Thank you very much, Englisch ist Quatsch!' (English is rubbish!).

To us it was quite funny, but he may have been protesting at having to learn English at school, and we could sympathize with him. Learning a foreign language at school is not the best way to learn it. It is far better to live in that country and learn the language there! As Tony and I did. But of course we can't all do that!

That same night in Travemuende Tony and I entered a local talent competition. We sang an 'Everly Brothers song, in harmony, 'All I Have To

Do is Dream', which won us first prize.

To be honest the competition wasn't strong! Maybe we shouldn't have been allowed to enter it, as we were not amateurs; but life is not fair sometimes!

The inevitable happened when we returned to the 'Flurschaenke' that evening and were asked to leave. The neighbours in the area had finally had enough; There had been too many police attendances because of the noise, and the old lady owner was at the end of her tether: not knowing how she was going to make Tony play more quietly.

Tony wasn't at all fazed when told we were no longer welcome. Of course we didn't argue we all saw this day coming – and were a bit surprised it took so long. We packed our things and left, heading back to the Reeperbahn.

Tony and I played together one more time at

the 'Kaiser Keller' – the club we had first played at on arrival in Hamburg in 1960. It was a great evening and brought back many happy memories. He then returned to the 'Top Ten' for more work with Polydor records.

The rest of the band, including myself, went our different ways. I took on a couple of labouring jobs in Hamburg, having changed my plans, and now intended to stay in Germany for Ingrid's sake. It was a mistake: resulting in some serious confrontations with German co-workers who mistakenly thought I was weak. I gave them a surprise, threatening the worse one with a shovel. I decided to give up the idea of staying in Germany with Ingrid, and would stick to my original plan of going back to the UK and setting up home in England.

I was then invited to play in a German band,

'The All Round Men' as singer and bassist, managed by Manfred Woitalla, who owned the 'Star Palast' in Lueneburg'. We played in and around Hamburg. After that I was invited to join a newly formed German band, the 'Bats', managed by Juergen Dankers; who later arranged what turned out to be the disastrous 'gig' at the 'Gruene Hoelle' Club in Berlin with Tony Sheridan.

'The Bats' was a good band with some talented young German musicians and singers. I was happy there. We toured the Berlin clubs, music halls and later played in Düsseldorf.

The American servicemen based in Berlin loved the 'Bats' and every year they hold an annual reunion, and talk about their great Berlin days. 'The Bats' were also invited by AFN (American Forces Network) to record some of our songs with them, which we did. I'm told the recordings are still available today on disc (although I can't find a copy!).

It was around this time that Tony wrote to me in Düsseldorf while I was playing there, inviting me to join him at the newly-opened 'Star Club' in Hamburg It was in May 1962 . At first I turned him down, as I was with the 'Bats' – but after they fell out with their manager, who seized their equipment, I wrote back to Tony telling him I was available, and he asked me to join him as soon as I could.

It will be good to be playing alongside Tony Sheridan my 'ole mate' again and was hearing much on the 'grapevine' about the, no expense spared, 'Star Club', which intended to bring only the top stars from America and elsewhere to the club.

The 'Star Club became one of the best European 'rock' venues ever and featured some unforgettable stars, mainly from America.

5. 'GRUENE HOELLE'

But before I tell you more about the fabulous 'Star Club' I must tell you about the 'gig' in Berlin with Tony, which ended in disaster, and could easily have ended our friendship.

As I said earlier it was Juergen Dankers, the 'Bats manager, who had organized the visit to the famous 'Gruene Hoelle' (Green Hell) club, which meant I would be backing my old mate, Tony again. Little did I know that in Berlin I would see another side to Tony Sheridan, a side I didn't really want to see, but for the sake of the story I must mention it – this time I wasn't prepared to sit back and let the incident go by without referring to it and doing something about it.

It all started innocently enough as the band set off by road, with all our equipment, towards the East German border at Marienborn, close to the Autobahn to Berlin, a city which had been partitioned since the end of the second world war. At the East German border we were given a frosty reception by the Vopos (Peoples Police). Once they had examined our passports and the music equipment in our van, they relaxed a little. We paid our fees and were granted visas for travel on the autobahn direct to Berlin. We were told not to stop or even to turn off the Autobahn for security reasons.

There were female 'Vopos' present at the checkpoint, too, and they were keen to know about the latest 'Twist' craze, and the rock and roll music sweeping across Europe, which of course they had very little knowledge about, other than having heard the music on their radios. The official line was that if the new music came from the west it must be decadent, whatever that meant! How can any kind of music be decadent?

'Show us how to do the twist?' said one of the female 'Vopo' officers at the control point.

'You really want us to show you ?' I asked, surprised at the idea; but she was serious.

'Yes please!' and soon we were all twisting around inside the the control box, the 'Vopos' trying their best to do it properly. It was a bit strange to see them stooping and gyrating about, while armed to the teeth, their machine guns flapping loosely over their shoulders.

'Like this?' they were asking, laughing and joking as they danced.

'That's it, you've got it!' They were human after all, and we left them happier than when we first arrived; we were waved off like film-stars towards the autobahn and Berlin.

It was early afternoon when we finally got there, and after first making ourselves comfortable at our destination, Tony and I spent the morning walking around the main

Charlottenberg area of Berlin close to the beautiful royal palace. The rest of the band, not as interested in history as Tony and I were, went for a drink.

Tony was at that time a keen collector of second world war German memorabilia, especially Nazi badges and medals and he hoped to find more in the second hand shops of Berlin which he did.

It was probably this interest in the war years (both of us were born during the 'Battle of Britain' year) that led us to the Berlin wall at 'Checkpoint Charlie'. There we could look across towards the rubble of what was once East Berlin, and see a modern-looking tram passing by on the east side of the wall, close to the border; all we could see behind it ,was the rubble of bombed buildings with large billboards in front. The boards were a futile attempt to hide the war damage from the eyes of the prosperous West Berlin, which had been mainly rebuilt.

Rebuilding took much longer in communist East Berlin than in West Berlin and the new tram was probably for propaganda purposes only: as there was never more than one tram to be seen on the East German side of 'Checkpoint Charlie' and there were no passengers on it.

'What do you think, Colin, shall we try and get

in?' Tony wanted to see East Berlin and so did I. 'We'll give it a go, but I don't hold out much hope, unless we tell them we're coming for a return visa'. The guards were a nasty-looking bunch and glared at us intently as we approached. We must have looked a bit out of the ordinary – not at all like tourists or bona fide visitors. Tony and I walked up to the sentry post next to the passport control office.

Outside of the office were huge blocks of concrete placed in the road, no doubt to stop vehicles attempting to crash through and escape to the west. The 'Vopos' continued looking us up and down as we approached, machine guns at the ready; then gestured to us, pointing and waving their guns towards the passport control office, behind the heavy concrete barriers. There we handed our passports in through a tiny bureau window.

'Weiter gehen' (Move on) said the person behind the window; but I wanted my passport back. 'Weiter gehen!' said the the 'Vopos' outside, gesturing with their machine guns again, and we moved on towards another window about ten feet further along where our passports were handed back to us, together with a notice instructing us to report to the Russian Embassy for an exit visa, which allowed us back through 'Checkpoint Charlie'. We needed a visa to travel on the East German autobahn back to West Germany. After carefully checking my passport I noticed the photo on one corner of the passport had been lifted and assumed the 'Vopos' were checking to see if anything was hidden behind it. Possibly microfilm.

We were moved on again and were now outside of the passport control area and inside East Berlin. The sight that met us on the east side of the Berlin

Wall was like a scene from the 'Blitz' on London. In every direction were bombed buildings and rubble. It looked as if the war had ended only a few days ago. Alongside the rubble was a small rail track with just one modern tram on it; The same one we had seen earlier from West Berlin going backwards and forwards along the track, and still without any passengers on board.

Before setting out from Hamburg we had already changed some West German Marks for East German ones, although East German marks were almost worthless in West Germany. We looked for a café and something to eat, but it was a hard job. We found only one. It would have to do, and we walked in and sat down. We were the only customers.

The place looked like a scene from 'Oliver Twist; Furniture was virtually non-existent and there was nothing to eat on show anywhere. We looked at each other, intending to get out of there as soon as possible. But a portly lady with a kind face came bustling towards us, we had left it too late..

'Guten Tag' she said, beaming pleasantly.

'Zwei Kaffee, Cappuccino' said Tony abruptly. The woman frowned;

'Cappu was?' (Cappu what!) She didn't understand and I told her it was a type of coffee,

'Hab ich nicht!' (I don't have it) she said to Tony, as gruffly as Tony had spoken to her.

I then asked her politely, in my best German, to give us whatever she had – as long as it was coffee. The kind lady waddled off muttering to herself. 'Diese Englander!' (These English!) She may have had only a few customers that day, but I'm sure Tony was the only one to have caused her any difficulty. He found it quite easy to upset people.

'Lets get out of here Colin, there's nothing to eat here'; Tony was getting frustrated.

'No, Tony, we've ordered now, we'll drink our coffee and then eat somewhere else.'

Eventually the coffee came, but neither of us could drink it. At the bottom of each of our cups was a thick, black sludge. On the top half of the cup was a watery substance that didn't look at all like coffee and was more like washing up water.

I called the lady back and paid the bill; we both stood up to leave. She looked blankly at us. We hadn't drunk our coffee! As we walked out I looked back to see her standing by the table looking at the money and then at us, before finally waddling off, back to her kitchen, waving her arms about and mumbling as she went.

After a long search we did find another café, but the food tasted awful there too. It was nothing like anything we'd eaten before, so we left that place as well.

We now set off to find the Russian Embassy, to get our visas for the return journey and stopped a passer-by to ask for directions. Once he heard us say, 'Russian Embassy', he gave us a horrified, suspicious look and quickly moved away.

We stopped at what appeared to be an official building: which was unlike any other building we had seen so far. Firstly it had been carefully repaired, whereas most buildings still showed at least some signs of bomb damage.

It wasn't the Russian Embassy, but it was classical in appearance, and could easily have been the kind of building we would expect an embassy or a consul to look like.

But it seemed to be abandoned. Tony walked up the wide stone steps and went straight inside, passing the huge Greek columns at the entrance. I followed nervously behind. What was he doing?

He didn't know what kind of place this was! It could have been the 'Vopo' Police Headquarters, and if caught in here we would surely both be in serious trouble!

Lining the walls in the huge hall inside were alcoves filled with classical statues, all depicting images of war and victory. Without needing to read what it said – which I couldn't as it was in Russian, I could see we were in a war memorial! There was still no sign of anyone around. Our footsteps echoed loudly around the enormous space, then Tony began shouting: to test the strength of the echo.

Then he began singing a rock 'n' roll song. I was horrified, it was so disrespectful. I was really worried; this was a place of remembrance, and we shouldn't be insulting it. If we were caught doing it, we would be arrested, locked up, and the key thrown away.

'Tony, shut up, you'll get us arrested!' Tony turned to me and smiled a cynical smile. He then stopped singing. I turned to leave and he followed, taking his time, and stopping at each of the classical stone carvings to carefully examine them.

We found the Russian Embassy which was close to the building we had just left, and walked in. It was alive with activity and, like embassies all over the world, every visitor is required to wait a long time before being seen. Its part of the ritual, maybe the staff liked the outside world to see their embassies filled with people. It makes them feel more important.

After serving our time in the waiting area, we now, at last, had our visas, allowing us to leave this miserable place and return to civilization on the other side of the wall.

On the way back towards what we thought was

the way to 'Checkpoint Charlie' we got lost. It was now getting late and we still had the gig to do that evening at the 'Gruene Hoelle'. Tony thought he knew better, but we seemed to be going round in circles. I saw a 'Vopo' in his green uniform carrying the obligatory machine gun, and standing close to a main road near a bridge.

'Stay there a minute Tony,' I'm going to get some directions; I didn't want any trouble.

'You're not going to talk to him are you, Colin?' This time it was Tony who was worried.

'Yes, I am' and walked over to him. He saw me coming and looked around nervously while Tony stayed where he was. The 'Vopo' knew straight away I was a foreigner.

I greeted him in German and he ignored me. I explained that we were English and had come from the Russian Embassy and were now trying to find 'Checkpoint Charlie'.

As soon as I mentioned 'Checkpoint Charlie' a look of horror crossed his face. Why? I don't know; He still hadn't said a word to me. Instead, he frantically began looking around again to see if anyone else was watching. As soon as he saw Tony standing watching us from across the street he quickly walked away, leaving me puzzled as to what was happening. Was it something I said? I had no idea.

Having discussed it later with my German friends in Hamburg the only thing they could suggest was that he was terrified to be seen talking to a foreigner, in case it looked like he was plotting an escape to the West, or helping someone else to do so. But Tony and I did find our way back to the 'Gruene Hoelle' in time, and by now it was late afternoon. We joined up with the rest of the band who were already on stage waiting for us.

Before starting we practised for a while: testing the speaker acoustics and microphone.

The club wasn't a big place and the audience was close to the stage; Tony liked it like that.

There was a buzz of excitement about the club and it quickly filled up. Everyone in Berlin had heard about Tony Sheridan – as had most of Germany. The early arrivals rushed to the front of the stage, making sure they would have the best places to watch their man play. It was the fans favourite place. Tony walked away off stage to go one last time to the toilet.

The club was now filled to breaking point with standing room only. Tony slowly made his way back to the stage, watched by the crowd. An infectious murmur accompanied him as he pushed his way through to the stage again. The atmosphere was now electric as he slowly and carefully went through his usual ritual of tuning and retuning his guitar, at the same time completely ignoring the excited, expectant audience. It was as if they weren't there.

Satisfied, he turned to us and nodded: which was both a question and a signal. The nod signalled he was ready, and the question was, were we? Happy that we were, he let rip with an explosion of emotive guitar-playing and sound: beginning with his much-loved standard, 'Skinny Minnie'

I could see the thrill on the faces of the audience, as Tony danced his famous dance, his voice rising stronger and stronger above the clapping and shouting of the happy audience.

Everything was going great, and that's when it all went to 'rats'. None of us were expecting what was about to happen. It came towards the end of the session, during another favourite number: 'What'd I say': a Ray Charles song where, during the chorus, Tony invited the audience to join in – the song was at its height and going great,

'Yea,' shouted Tony,

'Yea,' responded the audience,

'Yea,' shouted Tony once more,

'Yea,' repeated the audience, swaying happily, and holding their hands above their heads.

'Heil Hitler!' shouted Tony, and this time held his arm out in a Hitler salute. I was stunned as a strange hush descended on the audience. The mood immediately changed from one of celebration to one of shock, followed by looks of total disbelief. The band stopped playing. We looked at each other, hardly able to take in what had happened. What was he doing? We were in Berlin and the audience was German!

It was a death wish, the kind of thing only Tony Sheridan would do. No one expected it, and no one wanted it. What was the point of it anyway?

The band members looked at each other and the audience still shocked, were also looking at each other, open-mouthed: unable to understand what had happened. Meanwhile Tony stood motionless, still holding his arm out in the Hitler salute. It was weird.

Most of the young German audience present that fateful evening, hadn't even been born when Hitler came to power and now, here they were, on a great night out, shocked and unhappy. Having paid to see Tony Sheridan, they had instead been insulted, and publicly reminded of the sins of their forefathers. Tony's credibility had in an instantly disappeared, and gone from hero to zero. England, too, had much to be ashamed of in it's past history, as had many countries. But why remind everyone of all this stuff now? Gradually and quite slowly at first, the shocked audience moved towards the exits and left the club in silence, their heads hung low.

There was no protest, no shouts of anger, directed at Tony, just a noticeable deep silence, accompanied by the sound of chairs being scraped on the floor as the last of the deeply offended audience got up to leave. The club was now cold and empty: where moments ago it had been warm and friendly.

'Tony, what were you doing?' I demanded, as he finally lowered his arm and packed his guitar away. The band was now doing likewise, packing up, there was no point in carrying on. The gig had been ruined and I was fuming. Tony just smiled. I realised how angry I was. What did he expect would happen? What he did could not in any sense be called 'entertainment' and was totally uncalled-for. More annoyingly, I hadn't seen it coming.

'Tony!' (it was one of the waiters) 'There's a

telephone call from Juergen Dankers. Take it in the small bar'. Juergen Dankers had booked this 'gig', and it could be that he had been contacted by someone complaining about Tony.

'All right, I'm coming' and he walked out. I angrily finished packing my bass away and followed on behind. It wasn't that I didn't know that Tony was capable of doing something like this; I knew he was. I stood next to him at the bar while Tony sat on a Bar Stool talking on the phone to Juergen Dankers, telling him how wonderful the evening had been, and how much everyone in the packed club had enjoyed it. This made me even more angry.

I couldn't listen to any more and punched him in the mouth knocking him off his stool. A good old Irish-style fight followed in the bar, going this way and that. The waiters joined in: not to fight, but to try and separate us, but we didn't want to be separated, until finally I was pinned to the floor by three waiters unable to move, while Tony stood over me with a table raised high in the air, about to bring it crashing down on my head.

I was saved by two more waiters, who wrestled the table away from him, just when I thought I was a goner. The waiters still held me down, believing I was the guilty party. I suppose I was. But Tony was the real cause of it. I'm not usually a violent person.

Of course the show was over and we were never asked to play at the 'Gruene Hoelle' again. Yet another door had slammed shut on the career of Tony Sheridan.

Tony flew back to Hamburg, while I returned in the van by road. I don't think he even saw what happened as being one more nail in his professional coffin. Why did he do these things? I've no idea, but wish I did. But strangely it didn't affect our relationship at all, we still remained friends. It seemed nothing at all could pull us apart or come between us.

The odd thing about it was that Tony did actually feel remorse about certain things that happened in his life, and in later years he told me how much he regretted the fight we had in Berlin. It surprised me that he even remembered it. Up until then I didn't think he cared about the effects his behaviour had on other people, but deep down he really did care.

He would simply suppress his feelings and move on, instead of dealing with them.

He was a person full of strange contradictions. I often wondered how this came about. The answer may well have had something to do with his early life, but it was a life I knew little about. We came from two different worlds which were as far apart as our varied social backgrounds. Tony's in sophisticated Norwich, mine in London's docklands.

Before we got to know each other there was nothing we had in common, except for one thing – we were both 'war babies': children born during the war. We were also both confused, unhappy children. I had been evacuated to 'Barton Place', the Bishop of Exeter's house in Devon to avoid the bombing of London, and loved it so much that I never wanted to leave. On return to London I was unable to settle and ran away several times, trying to find my true home at Barton Place again.

But Tony's memories were the opposite; His mother had placed him in a children's home in Norwich, which he hated. He felt abandoned by his mother who had left him there. And as she walked away, he remembers screaming at her to come back. His memories of it were still vivid.

But many children are damaged by war; that's what wars do. Like me he found it impossible to forget those times, and what had happened to us. We were both glad,when as teenagers, we found a way to escape the misery and bitter memories of childhood, which had hurt us so deeply.

But it wasn't all bad, Tony's mother did come back, and she did take him away from the children's home. The family had since moved to 34 York Street in Norwich, a pleasant tree-lined road filled with smart Victorian houses: with large sash windows and neat gardens, situated close to the City Centre. But once home Tony felt it was too late to put things right; he still resented what had happened to him as a child and of being made to live with strangers, and he secretly carried that anger and bitterness with him for much of his life, before finally being able to talk about it to others.

Tony's talent would, from then on, be mixed

with bitterness and lead him to secretly run away to London with his skiffle group 'The Saints'. They had a dream to become part of the London music scene and together boarded the night-time 'Milk Train' to London.

Tony left a note for his mother, which he asked his sister Kathy to pass on to her. Tony's mother must have been upset when she read it. She was a fine pianist herself, and the violin lessons she had arranged for Tony with 'Elsie', his music teacher, at the Cathedral Close, Norwich, together with his leadership of the school orchestra, may have in her view, been wasted. But they had not, and although Tony wasn't to become the 'Yehudi Menuhin' his mother had hoped for, he did succeed in becoming a great singer/guitarist and songwriter. But of course, rock and roll was not his mothers kind of music, and it may not have been any consolation to her that this is the music her son had chosen to perform.

The war left behind many confused children on both sides, and probably many thousands who felt as Tony did, but there are many different stories to tell about the sacrifices made by our loving, caring, parents and the heartache they had lived through, while trying to make sure their children were safe.

The only difference between our generation and our elders was that we didn't blame the Germans of our own age, for what had happened to us. They, too, had suffered greatly, and through no fault of their own. All we can do is to make sure it never happens again. But my eyes are not blinkered; I'm sure it will happen again. Human nature is too unstable to change so quickly, and despite the two terrible German wars we have still not learnt anything.

After the surreal experience at the 'Gruene

Hoelle' we returned to Hamburg and luckily few people, except the agents and club owners, knew anything about what had happened in Berlin. Tony never mentioned it to me again; except the part about the fight, which, as I said, he wished hadn't happened. But it really didn't affect our relationship at all, which surprised me greatly. Usually, after a fight, a friendship ends, but ours didn't. He remained who he was, and so did I. We still argued and differed in our opinions, but having spoken our minds, that was the end of it. Another fight was out of the question.

Back in Hamburg Tony was increasingly involved at the 'Top Ten' and had made more recordings with the Beatles at Polydor records. Some of the songs had already been recorded with the 'Jets' (now renamed the 'Beat Brothers') before the Beatles had arrived in Hamburg, and it was Bert Kaempfert who had produced them. As I have already said, I was there playing and recording with Tony and the 'Jets' on the first Sheridan albums. But Bert Kaempfert couldn't cope with someone like Tony, nor did he know which songs suited Tony best. But with the arrival of 'The Beatles' – who by now had released their first single, 'Love Me Do', and their first LP, 'Please Please Me', it made sense for Polydor and Tony to release some of the old recordings that the 'Jets' ('Beat Brothers') had made earlier, together with new material from 'The Beatles', thereby helping to make the people at Polydor famous and to cash in on the earlier recordings made during Tony's association with 'The Beatles'.

The tables were turned and 'The Beatles' had now become the dominant force at Polydor records. Tony Sheridan needed to give way to them, and rightly so. It was 'The Beatles' who were raising British popular music to new heights with the earlier help of Tony Sheridan's experience and input, as well as his advice and guidance, which had helped 'The Beatles' greatly in those early days – something I doubt they will ever deny. They had called him 'The Teacher' but he was also their 'Mentor' and having listened they learnt well. Nor did their collaboration end when 'The Beatles became famous (as Tony later told me in his letters).

The difficulty Polydor had was they were slow to realize what an outstanding group they had in their studios, and so didn't re-sign 'The Beatles' under contract when they had the chance to do so. And even when they did realize their talent, 'The Beatles' had already left Germany, leaving the door open for another record company, and the many talented recording experts in England, to step in and guide 'The Beatles'. The technical people, together with a great manager (Brian Epstein), played an enormous part in making them world stars.

Not for the first time Tony Sheridan had missed the boat and others had leap-frogged over him, having first benefited from Tony's teachings. Fate can often be a cruel companion, but that's show-biz, folks! I don't blame Tony at all for later doing his best to salvage something from his great, and important, contribution to rock and roll, both in Hamburg, the UK and in many parts of the world. Fame arrived too slowly for Tony Sheridan. But it had owed much to the publicity 'The Beatles' gave him, which Tony much appreciated.

Tony could have achieved much more, and could have done it without the help of 'The Beatles', but that's now in the past, Tony obviously didn't want it. That's the only conclusion I can come to. He would abide by his own hidden agenda and go his own way.

He once wrote to me saying, *"joint recordings and four months of intensive work with 'The Beatles' (in Hamburg) had attracted the attention of manager Brian Epstein but I had resisted the offer to return with them to England, with no regrets"*.

Tony clearly felt he didn't need the fame of working with 'The Beatles', and of course they didn't need him now either. Tony's career was a catalogue of missed opportunities. This was simply one more. He did what he did and moved on – that was the story of his life.

He was, in my view, a tortured soul: he just wanted to play and sing and to do so by being himself. He liked recognition, but didn't need it. The nearest hint he gave to wanting fame was when he told me about going into a record shop and buying a copy of his own single, 'My Bonnie'.

He told me how he walked out of the shop and turned the record over and over in his hands, examining every bit of it. But that was all, he then put it away and moved on.

The record was, for him, already in the past. But he did receive recognition, and the ardour of his many fans. In 1984/85 Tony told me he had received a gold album achievement award for his work by the music industry.

I know he was proud of his achievements, for which he had been recognized. He was also proud to have taught others what he knew, and as I have said, had always done so willingly.

But despite his talent, Tony, when 'being himself', was not acceptable to those around him, especially the managers. He could also shock his fans by his behaviour, and in the end many of them had no time for him at all. It was the outrageous side of his nature that cost him so dearly. It was also the most mysterious. Why did an intelligent, well-educated guy do what he did? No one has ever been able to answer that question, and nor could I.

We lost contact a bit during 'The Beatles' years in Hamburg, but every now and again I would receive a letter from him, written from the heart, and I would visit him at his home in Seestermuehe, northern Germany, where he lived with Anna and their family. I was also invited there for Tony's surprise 70th birthday party. Together again we talked non-stop.

It was during one of my many visits that I told him about my own family's Irish origins, and that my original surname was Crowley (an Irish name from County Cork) and not Crawley. He was for some reason (probably because of his own Irish connections) deeply moved, and got quite excited, promising to send me a hand-painted parchment of the 'Crowley' family Coat of arms. Tony was by then heavily involved in Heraldry and had been accepted as a member of the artistic 'Heraldry' Association, which specialized in the painting of family coats of arms; Tony had, himself already created some wonderful work.

Many didn't know that Tony Sheridan had been a student at the Norwich college of Art, in Norfolk before rock 'n' roll came along, a music which compelled him to quickly change direction as it did for many of us. In fact the 60's, as we already know, changed everything.

6. 'STAR CLUB'

Let's go back to the invitation to join Tony at the newly opened 'Star Club' as the resident band, the 'Star Combo'. I did so in May 1962. Members of the band were: Tony Sheridan, Roy Young, (vocals and keyboards), Ricky Barnes, saxophone, a stand-in drummer (soon to be replaced by Johnny Watson) and lastly myself on bass-guitar.

Our time there was a fantastic one. Long ago the 'Star Club' had been a theatre with seats for many hundreds, the main hall sloped downwards towards the wide stage with its heavy draped curtains. During that first evening there was a constant buzz about the place.

The club was already full when we arrived and the atmosphere was electric. Many of the fans made camp in front of the stage, as German fans like to do. We hadn't rehearsed – as Tony didn't believe in rehearsing – he believed in 'feeling the music' and taking it from there. At the same time he didn't tolerate any 'duff' notes, but despite Tony being unhappy with the drummer, and often needing to 'correct' him, we did reach new heights when playing at the 'Star Club'.

There is something special about a band that is playing tightly together – sometimes it is as if the music and the musicians, merge to become one complete entity. But we were still looking for a better drummer; It was the only thing missing. But despite this the club was filled every night with an enormous enthusiastic crowd, which danced and cheered non-stop at everything they saw and heard. We played to a strict timetable, which annoyed Tony – he liked to start and finish only when he was quite ready. The timetable had to be that way, to make sure the audience got a fair share of every artist appearing on that particular night. The artists, too, needed to know exactly when they were due on stage.

Our job at the 'Star Club', apart from completing our own 'sets', was to back visiting artists who had arrived at the club with no band of their own. We were prepared for anything, thanks to the guidance of Tony, who made sure the 'Star Combo' did credit to the artists we had admired since we were wide-eyed teenagers. None of us ever expected to see so many of our American rock 'n roll heroes together under one roof.

There was a definite 'something' in the air the first night we played, which lasted the whole evening. It seemed everybody who was anybody in the rock 'n roll world, was there that evening when the 'Star Combo' made its début and played together as a band.

Tony still wasn't happy with our drummer, and

approached Johnny Watson, who had arrived with another visiting band, 'Tex Roberg and the Graduates' from Southampton; Johnny was something special, and Tony wanted him in the 'Star Combo'. He made him an offer he couldn't refuse! Johnny agreed to join us, but 'Tex Roberg and the Graduates' were not happy, even when Tony offered our drummer in exchange as well. But there were no contracts involved, and Johnny Watson chose to join us of his own free will; That's how things were done in those days – Informally.

'Tex Roberg and the Graduates' were to have the small satisfaction of being the band to open the show on the first evening that 'The Beatles' arrived. Who went on stage first was decided by the toss of a coin, which Tex won, and 'The Beatles' had to wait for 'Tex and the Graduates', to finish before they could go on. Which helped make up, in a small way, for us 'stealing' Johnny Watson from them.

I remember my time with the 'Star Combo' for another reason too. The weirdest thing happened. It may sound odd to talk about a rock 'n roll band 'swinging'. Rock bands do swing sometimes, when all is going well, and it means just that: 'As one' or 'tight-together'.

It is a term given to jazz bands, or events that are blending perfectly together, and we can even refer to certain sexual events which I won't go into! But these are not the kinds of 'swinging' I'm talking about. It was all a complete mystery – that is, until it happened to me.

As I mentioned earlier, Tony was on top of his game and everyone in the band was playing together as one. The crowd was loving it, and we sounded great. Then it happened. Halfway through a Ray Charles number I felt myself being spookily lifted off my feet, not violently or quickly, but slowly and gently. I rose serenely up off the stage and came to a stop, hovering about three feet above the stage floor. I wasn't afraid, just confused as to what could possibly be going on. At the same time having a wonderful euphoric feeling of togetherness and pleasure, and a vague suspicion it was happening through the music.

But how or why it came about I really don't know, as it had never happened to me before.

Anyone reading this might say, 'I bet he was high on something', but I know I wasn't. I don't do drugs, never have done, and don't normally drink until after the show – no alcohol is allowed on stage during performances.

It was weird, and the whole thing lasted only about a minute or two. In that time I wondered why no one seemed to have noticed that I was up in the air, or saw me come down again and settling in the same spot I had started from.

The number ended and I turned to Johnny Watson in the short break before the next number,

'Did you feel that, too, Johnny? I lifted up off the stage!' I was quite excited about it.

'Yea, Col, I felt it', he said smiling, as though it was quite a normal thing to have occurred, but, as I said, it had never happened to me before. After our set I spoke some more to Johnny about it. I was curious to find out why he didn't find it unusual, and whether or not he knew what caused it, as it felt so real.

'Tell me more about that lifting off the stage thing, Johnny. Has it happened to you before?' Johnny answered in a way that made it seem like no big deal.

'A couple of times, yea, it happened to me in two other bands, we called it 'swinging'. Why do you ask – did you like it?' He was now grinning broadly, realizing it was my first time. But seeing that I was deadly serious about it, Johnny explained it a bit more,

'I don't know what causes it, except it seems to happen to the whole band at exactly the same time, but only when the band is playing perfectly together, as we did tonight'.

But it was still a mystery. I knew Johnny didn't take drugs, and never saw him drink alcohol. I believed him. As for me I did drink – sometimes too much, but as I said, I hadn't had a drink at all that evening when the 'swinging' occurred. I wanted to be 'on the music', with no silly mistakes or 'duff' notes.. From then on, when someone spoke about 'swinging', it had a whole new meaning for me. On stage I always waited, hoping it would happen again, but it never did. But at least I did feel better just knowing Johnny Watson had experienced it too, and knew what I was talking about.

The 'Star Club was every bit the success everyone expected it to be. We saw the great rock stars from America, the ones we had grown up with from our youth, it was a fabulous time, like meeting up with long-lost friends. Fats Domino was there, beaming and unchanged since those early days, as he sang once more his classic, 'Blueberry Hill.'

Little Richard, put on a great show as he climbed up on top of his grand piano screaming out 'Lucille' in his own Gospel style. Jerry Lee Lewis was there, too, his hands just a blur as he effortlessly ran his fingers up and down the piano keyboards occasionally lifting his leg and tickling or stamping on the ivories with his feet while purring, growling and screaming into the mike as he sang 'Johnny B Goode'; exactly as we remembered it all those years ago.

Tony's hero, Ray Charles, was there, too. Tony was beside himself, as we all were. It was such a powerful occasion, like being in rock 'n roll heaven! But it will never happen again.

All the kids of our era have memories of the time rock 'n roll first arrived in England and turned our boring lives upside down, and now Bill Haley himself was here at the 'Star Club': reminding us again of the time he and his band had caused riots all over England.

Tony and I saw it happen – when 'Rock around the Clock' sent the teenage crowds wild, hopping and bopping in the aisles of our local cinemas, where once they had sat rigidly in neat silent rows and behaved themselves. Doing strictly as they were told to do.

Outside in the streets, police cars were being turned over just for the pure joy of it. Revolution was in the air, not a political one, but more like one generation against another. The young were determined to break free from the shackles of their staid elders.

Many more of our early heroes appeared at the 'Star Club' during its heyday, and our time as resident band – far too many to mention. The 'Star Combo' also became Gene Vincent's backing band during his UK, European and Israel tours and I was with them.

Joey Dee and the 'Starliters' (Peppermint Twist) were there, too. Joey Dee was so impressed with Tony, he wanted to take him to the famous 'Peppermint Lounge' in New York and sponsor him in America. Tony inexplicably declined without giving a reason, but Joey Dee together with the 'Starliters' did help with the vocal backing on one of our LP recordings with Polydor (Ruby Baby) having offered to do it for free – which they did.

The 'Star Combo' backed both Brenda Lee and Tommy Roe, at the 'Star Club' as they had arrived without a band. Tommy Roe had world-wide hits with 'Dizzy' and 'Wild Thing'.

Brenda Lee had many hits in the 60's, and I loved her powerful and sincere voice. Lastly and the most famous band of all, 'The Beatles' came to the 'Star Club', having appeared there more than once while we were there. They were truly great times and it was all happening there, at the 'Star Club'.

All the memories, and all the songs of our youth, came flooding back, again and again, and now we could hear them being sung in front of us by the original artists! There could never be another club like the 'Star Club' – as many of these artists are no longer with us.

But I'm sure no other club-owner could ever afford to pay the costs of having so many great original artists appearing on the same bill, in the same place and on the same night!

It's all changed now, and it's a shame that so many stars of today are being 'manufactured' by others, rather than being allowed to keep their own individual talents and originality; Once they become,'doctored' their individuality is lost forever. Nobody ever told Elvis, Little Richard, or Jerry Lee Lewis how to perform or how to sing, they just did it!

We are all unique human beings and learn these things in our own way, which we could.

At the 'Star Club' I remember seeing Ray Charles and his band waiting in the wings to go on stage, he was next on after the 'Star Combo'. We were having a great time and Tony gave a terrific show again. When we came off, one of the stage hands told me that while we were playing, Ray Charles had asked him who it was singing on stage,

'That was Tony Sheridan,' said the stage hand.

'He's good, very good' said Ray, which was great praise from one of Tony's great idols!

Mixed in with all the well-known artists from Amcrica were other British and German bands: 'Gerry and the Pacemakers', 'King Size Taylor', 'Joe Brown', 'The Liver Birds', 'The Big Six', 'The Rattles', 'Johnny Kid and the Pirates', Vince Taylor, (a showman to rival Elvis, and just as good looking, but sadly he wasn't a good singer). There were many more, and they will all be remembered whenever people talk about the 'Star Club' in Hamburg.

There was one act I remember most of all, although he was only on stage for a few minutes! It was 'Screaming Lord Such'. How could I ever forget him? He arrived at the 'Star Club' as an unknown, except to a small minority of English bands. I myself had never heard of him! But once seen, never forgotten. Tony and I were in the audience at the time, curious about this new arrival, and said to be a 'bit weird'. The 'Star Combo' wasn't due on stage until later, and we wanted to see how weird Screaming Lord Such really was.

The audience was quiet as the curtains slowly opened, revealing a darkened, moody stage. To add to the mood was an awful sound of loud, screeching music, accompanied by a frantic and blinding array of flashing coloured lights. When at last the the stage curtain was fully opened, there was no one there – nor could we see the band responsible for making the spooky sounds. All that confronted the audience was a lone coffin raised up on two wooden supports and covered with what looked like a bloodstained cloth.

The volume of the now hysterical music grew louder and more frantic, the stage lights flashed even more wildly in the gloom. Somewhere on stage, Screaming Lord Such's band ('The Savages') were still not visible, but the increasing volume of their guitars now suggested they were certainly there and creating the unbearable rock/horror sound. The 'Star Club' was full and the audience was at first hushed and curious, as an eerie and deathly silence descended on everyone. Some, mostly the women, were open-mouthed and holding their hands over their ears, frantically trying to exclude the awful sounds.

Baffled by this strange show, the men and boys in the audience, though shocked and confused, tried to stoically take it all in their stride, pretending to know what was about to happen. Others stared at each other with looks of amazement and tense anticipation at what what was going on, and why all the drama. Then the lid of the coffin began to open as if by itself.

No one had seen anything like it. The crowd expected a rock band and instead was getting this creepy show! The weird sounds and loud music carried on for a few more minutes and the flashing lights picked up speed now seemingly out of control.

The heavy lid of the coffin was now fully open, but no one appeared. The suspense was building and the waiters stopped what they were doing and look at each other with bewildered expressions. Meanwhile the coffin stayed open, but still nothing was happening.

We all waited for what seemed ages. The tension, mixed with curiosity, was now becoming unbearable, but everyone stayed to watch – Transfixed. No one dared leave and miss out on what might turn out to be something tremendously cool and worth seeing.

After a deathly hush there followed a tremendously loud crash, which made people jump. Then a misty white cloud arose from inside the coffin, followed by a horrific, half-vampire figure, dressed in a black cape and black top hat, and what appeared to be blood dripping from its mouth. It leaped out of the coffin and onto the stage and ran, screaming loudly, towards the audience, wielding an enormous, wicked-looking axe above his head, which looked like a real one and probably was!

Moving at speed it left the stage and ran into the audience, still with the same blood-curdling cries, grimacing horribly and waving the axe around in a threatening way. Huge parts of the audience, mainly the girls, rushed for the exits with piercing screams, covering their heads with their hands. This was not what they were expecting.

'What the fuck is that!?', said Tony, standing next to me with a huge grin on his face. But I saw a dangerous situation arising as panic infected more and more of the audience. Those girls, who were not frightened before, were now running for their lives or hiding under the tables, not knowing what was going on. The German crowd had never seen anything like this before in their lives – nor had Tony and I.

Screaming Lord Such was now halfway down the aisle of the club, still brandishing the axe above his head. The crowd parted to let him through as he swept everyone away in front of him. There was pandemonium and still no one had tried to stop him.

Many more of the panicking throng now mostly the younger men, who had so far stood their ground, were now also running away, pushing and bullying their way down the aisles towards the exits, closely followed by Screaming Lord Such, still brandishing the axe above his head. But two quick-thinking waiters stopped him with really good rugby tackles – one waiter on each leg – as he came running by, bringing him crashing down.

The last I saw of him was being dragged through the club by his feet and ejected through the club's 'emergency exit' door. That was the end of Screaming Lord Such. His two week show was cancelled the next day.

I met him later by chance in the street outside and we talked about what had happened. He told me his act 'hadn't worked' and he was now broke, and would I like to buy a ring from him? I made my apologies as he was a bit pushy, and wouldn't take no for an answer.

He kept bringing the price of the ring down, but for some reason I didn't feel sorry for him. If he had asked me, I would have given him some money, or bought him something to eat, but he didn't, and I never saw him again. His band, 'The Savages', stayed on in Germany and played at the 'Star Palast', in Lueneburg, managed by Manfred Woitalla, who had previously managed one of my previous German bands, the 'All Round Men'.

Screaming Lord Such returned to the UK and became a politician, forming the 'Official Monster Raving Loony Party'. But sadly on 16th June 1991, he hanged himself following the death of his mother the previous year. There are some things we are never able to deal with.

They were truly great times in those early days of the clubs in Hamburg, and wherever our band played, and The Beatles' were in town, they would not be far away – watching and learning from Tony, who had gladly spent a great amount of time with them.

This association was to continue long after 'The Beatles' collaboration with him in Germany had ended and they had returned to the UK. According to Tony's letters, his long music association with them was to continue for many more years but Tony never bragged about it.

'The Beatles' were a varied bunch of characters, although, apart from Ringo I had spent very little time with them when we were in Germany, except when they were appearing at the 'Star Club' where the 'Star Combo' was resident band. I tended to spend most of my free time either with Johnny Watson, or with my girlfriend, Ingrid, at her parents house. Only occasionally was I with Tony (and then only when he was not on walkabouts!).

I got on well with George Harrison and Stuart Sutcliffe and of course Ringo, who had played with us in 'The Jets' before returning to Liverpool.

George was very easy to get on with – being uncomplicated and polite. I had a lot of time for Stuart, too. He was after all, a fellow bass player and playing at the same venue as we were. It was quite natural for us to be standing by the stage and talking about music and bass-guitars.

Somehow Stuart seemed to have separated himself from the rest of 'The Beatles', and would often be standing apart from them, in a space of his own. I noticed the same with Pete Best, and both looked like they didn't fit in, and were rarely seen talking to the others,

I liked them all really but preferred people with quiet unassuming manners and more interesting conversations. But it wasn't too difficult to see who the main motivating forces were within 'The Beatles'.

On one occasion Stuart and I were once more talking at the foot of the stage in the 'Star Club' where he was again alone,waiting to go on. I noticed he had piano strings on his bass guitar, something I had never seen any other bass guitarist do before. I was surprised, as obviously they were far too long and left four large conspicuous coils dangling from the neck of his bass. I asked him about them and why he wanted to use piano strings.

'I don't know, Colin, I just think they have a great sound'.

'But why don't you cut them down, they're too long?'

'I'm not yet sure how much more they're going to stretch' he said. But even though I thought it was an interesting idea, I wasn't tempted to try the same myself, and still haven't seen any other bass player use piano strings on a bass guitar!

It was around this time I was looking to change my 'Hofner' violin bass for a Gibson.

The Hofner finger-board was not that good. I found the strings easily went out of tune, (no matter what make of strings I put on it!). The weak tuning pegs could have been the problem, but for me the Hofner simply wasn't up to the job.

Word must have got round that I was selling it, possibly either Stuart Sutcliffe or Tony Sheridan had mentioned it to Paul, but it was actually a German guy who told me that Paul McCartney was interested in buying my Hofner from me. He even told me how much Paul was prepared to pay for it! I thought it a bit strange that Paul should ask about it via a third party, and not ask me himself. We were, after all, both playing at the 'Star Club'!

I just felt that if Paul really wanted to buy it, he could ask me himself, and so left it at that, thinking no more about it. I heard nothing more from Paul and sold the Hofner to a young up-and-coming German bassist for less money than Paul was willing to pay for it.

I then went back to Steinways music store in the centre of Hamburg, (the same place I had bought my Hofner violin bass), and put down a deposit on a beautiful Gibson solid body 'Les Paul' – the total cost was 235 marks (in November 1962). (Serial No 23826) which I later sold in England for £90 – to pay for our son's first bike. I later heard Paul had bought his own 'Hofner' bass and thereby made the violin bass world famous.

It would be nice to get that awesome Gibson Les Paul bass back again. Tony loved it too, and liked to play it himself, whenever he got the chance, but he wasn't that good! He was just as aggressive with a bass as he was with the drums! He did have great dexterity and feeling when playing his own guitar, but this didn't extend to his playing other instruments!

But at least he didn't break the Gibson, as Vince Taylor's bass player did, after I had kindly lent it to him when he played at the 'Star Club', (after he had damaged his own).

Sometimes, after finishing playing for the evening at the 'Star Club', I would go out with Johnny Watson for something to eat and then for a walk. Johnny liked to go to the 'Spiel Halle' opposite the 'Star Club' where he would thrash a few young German players at 'table-top football'. Johnny's lightning reactions and tactical skill were unbelievable and the local German boys badly wanted to beat him. There was usually a crowd of them around the table whenever Johnny was playing. I suspect they hoped to see him lose a game. But he didn't.

Tony came along once, and we both gave Johnny a game (two against one), but he made us both look incredibly clumsy. I suppose it helped that Johnny was a drummer and drummers need to have supple wrists, but Johnny Watson was truly something else!

Come to think of it I don't remember stories of anyone ever beating him, either English or German. His speed of play and lightning reactions, were just too much for everyone.

Meanwhile Tony continued living the high life elsewhere with his 'friends', doing things that didn't interest me at all. I never asked Tony what he got up to, but I suspect it included things none of us should be doing.

Johnny and I enjoyed the simple life, and simple pleasures, while Tony, always the wild boy, (a 'chancer' as we call them in London) lived his life on a slippery slope. It always amazed me how Tony and I could be good friends and able to ignore our differences, no matter what. But we were, and nothing ever changed.

He was able to cause trouble anywhere – and did so even at the 'Lila Lerchenfeld' an annual students festival held at the Hamburg College of Art.

The band was invited to play there. Tony and a German fan who had come with us ended up in a fight with some students and some got hurt. We were asked to leave, and of course never invited back there again. It was this kind of behaviour that kept most would-be managers away from Tony Sheridan.

At times my hectic life did get a bit too much, and I longed for a bit of peace and quiet,
Sometimes, without anyone knowing it, I would sneak into the usually empty St Josephs Catholic church in the 'Grosse Freiheit' opposite the 'Kaiser

Keller' and just sit there for a while, saying a prayer and asking myself what life was all about, and where was I going, and how I could change things. I made sure no one knew I went there. Not even Tony knew.

I always left that peaceful church feeling much better. One of the reasons I liked Tony was that he was a deeply spiritual person, which he hid well. We would often talk about spiritual things, and discussed his seeking guidance from a different source than mine.

To him Buddhism was the way. We agreed that there were many pathways to God.

I was continuing to spend more and more time with Ingrid's family in Lurup, and spending most nights there, much to the annoyance of Johnny, as he was now left very much on his own in St.Pauli, whereas usually, when our stint at the 'Star Club' had finished he and I would team up. As I said earlier Johnny was not into drink or drugs. He saved his money.

On increasingly rare occasions Tony, Johnny and I would sit down together at the nearby 'Gretal & Alfons' bar in the Grosse Freiheit and talk. We talked a lot, and Johnny always had interesting stories to tell tell about his early teens, and how he had started out in his music career. It was an unusual one as Johnny first began playing in a rock band as lead-guitarist, playing in different Southampton rock bands, including 'The Graduates' with Tex Roberg. Johnny knew that as a lead-guitarist or singer he had more street-cred, and 'pulled' the most girls, and would thereby have one of the most important positions in the band.

But Johnny soon discovered he was born to play drums and not guitar. Nor was he born to be a singer and so, like many aspiring 'provincials', including Tony Sheridan, he made his way to Soho and the London cellar clubs, during the early days of British rock.

He began playing gigs here and there, wherever he could find work, and was often hungry. He also did 'session' work', answering advertisements to do 'one off' jobs, such as TV advertising which by their nature, were short-lived. He needed a permanent job.

Johnny told Tony and me how, when once looking for work, he saw an advertisement in a London newspaper, inviting drummers to an audition with Tony Crombie, the great London Jazz drummer, band leader and composer, who later, after rock 'n' roll arrived in England, formed a rock 'n' roll band, 'The Rockets'. They released the very first British rock 'n' roll record, 'Teach you to Rock'.

Johnny had always been a bold character and a 'chancer'. His confidence was permanently sky high. He believed he always had a chance of getting whatever job he applied for, even if it meant 'winging it'. Which is a way of appearing confident (and competent), even if you don't have the slightest idea what the job you have applied for requires you to do.

But Johnny badly needed the work and so 'went for it': not knowing he will be required to to read drum music (which he couldn't). But Johnny was already a master of knowing how to 'wing it' and not be discovered. He would quickly cover up any mistakes with a little improvisation, skulduggery or bare-faced cheating, depending on how much he wanted the job. But you need to be an expert to find your way past a master drummer like Tony Crombie: as Johnny was to find out.

He arrived at the hall where Tony Crombie had

assembled all the musicians. Each of them was handed their music, according to the instrument they were playing, which included the drum music, which Tony Crombie gave to Johnny.

" It was a wide scroll of sheet music with squiggly bits which looked like a plate of spaghetti. I looked at it and straight away put it to one side, It was no use to me, and when the practice session started I simply listened to what was being played and found a suitable drum-piece that fitted in with what everyone else was doing". But Tony Crombie was no mug and straight away shouted,

'Stop!' Stop!' and came over to me and looked at my drum music'.

'What the hell are you playing? Show me where you are with the music!' Johnny and Tony Crombie looked at the drum music together, while all the time Johnny pretended he knew exactly what he was playing, and where he was with the music, but in fact still couldn't read any part of it.

By coming over to him Crombie had given Johnny a good idea of what he wanted him to play, without Johnny needing to read the music. The band started again from the beginning. 'Stop!' 'stop!' Stop!' shouted Tony Crombie, and rushed over to Johnny again, who told us how he then put on his innocent look; but this time Tony Crombie was really angry,

'Johnny, tell me, what the fuck are you playing? 'Show me on the music where you are'. That's how it went on with Johnny pretending he was in control of the drum music, knowing exactly what to play, and Tony Crombie knowing that he wasn't and didn't.

Johnny was in trouble. Tony Crombie was becoming more and more frustrated by Johnny who was continuing to play what he thought would fit, instead of following the music. At last the piece was finished and it sounded good. Tony Crombie walked over to Johnny afterwards and had a quiet word with him,

'You didn't have a fucking clue about that drum music, did you, Johnny?'

"No, not really", said Johnny honestly, "But did you like it?" smiling innocently as he spoke. Tony Crombie stared at him for a while and smiled,

'I did, Johnny, you've got a lot of natural talent and I'm giving you the job'.

Johnny was later given a lot more work with Tony Crombie as well as getting valuable drum lessons and coaching from a master drummer, and soon, Johnny became his regular supporting drummer, taking the great Tony Crombie's place on tour whenever a second drummer was needed.

The only problem now was that whenever they

went on tour together there was usually only one drum kit on stage, which Tony Crombie would always set up to suit himself.

This meant that the drum kit 'set-up' had to remain unaltered, even when Johnny was playing it. Tony Crombie's set-up was different to everyone else's. In the end Johnny got used to it, and even when Johnny was no longer playing in Tony Crombie's band, and had his own drum kit, he would set the drums up in the same way that Tony Crombie did.

It was a habit that never left him and later, whenever Johnny played someone else's drums he would change them round to suit himself using the Crombie style set-up, much to the annoyance of the drums owner, who had to change his drums back again afterwards.

Of course Johnny learnt a lot from Tony Crombie and as a result was acknowledged by all who knew about these things as a great rock 'n' roll drummer.

Johnny told me it was Tony Crombie who taught him most about drums and the drum rhythms; It helped that Johnny was once a lead guitarist, and had changed over to drums quite early in his rock 'n' roll career. He understood lead guitar and Tony' Sheridan's rhythms; Johnny became a top drummer on the British rock 'n' roll scene.

Tony Sheridan had spotted Johnny's talent in the 'Star Club' immediately, and now he was the 'Star Combo's drummer. Later, 'The Beatles' approached Johnny about joining them, but he told them he was happy where he was, with us at the 'Star Combo'.

I never saw another drummer as technically gifted as Johnny Watson. I noticed that whenever we were out together he was constantly practising rhythms by tapping them out on his knee, or on the edge of the table while he talked. He seemed to be doing it subconsciously. Drumming was in his blood.

He was also a great guy and we became good friends. It was he who brought me to live in Southampton, as Ingrid wouldn't have liked my scruffy home in the docklands of London.

While at the 'Star Club', and earlier the 'Top Ten', Tony and I noticed something strange about Germans and German club owners, which I hadn't noticed before. It was their insistence on wearing uniforms. It seems as if every trade and organisation in Germany had a uniform:even the chimney-sweeps and carpenters wore them – the carpenters looked like the Cisco Kid with their black wide-brimmed hats, fancily decorated waistcoats and bell-bottomed trousers. All they now needed now, was to turn up for work on a horse!

The uniform problem started when we moved to the 'Top Ten' from the 'Kaiser Keller', which I have already talked about, and now, once again, while we were resident band in the 'Star Club', we were again issued with uniforms with 'Star Combo' emblazoned on our jackets. But to be fair to the 'Star Club' bosses, we did look unusually smart, and were also playing the best music of our lives, which compensated for the strict requirement to wear uniforms. But the English are a nation of individuals. Uniforms are not always required!

7. GENE VINCENT

It was about this time that the 'Star Combo' was asked by Don Arden, the famous British manager, to back Gene Vincent on a tour of the UK in 1962. Tony Sheridan would be the supporting singer and lead guitarist. The tour started in London. Straight away we noticed that Gene was not what he used to be, and now just a shadow of what he once was. Yes, the audience loved him, and he didn't let them down, but they couldn't see what we a could see, Gene looked terribly tired and jaded.

It was as if he was just going through the motions. His heart wasn't in it. Don't get me wrong, Tony helped him out, and did much of the singing on the tour. It started in London where Gene gave as much as he could, and the audiences loved him. It was as if every Gene Vincent fan was there

We moved on to Portsmouth (home of the Royal Navy) where Gene got a wonderful reception. He had served in the American Navy, and decided to start the show. Tony took over when Gene got tired. It was a good arrangement, and worked very well. The tour was so far a great success.

Our last show of this particular tour was at Haverfordwest in Wales, and it was there the mike-stand came apart while Gene was on stage singing. It was far worse than it looked, as it meant Gene couldn't use the mike-stand to support himself and take the pressure off his injured leg, as he had needed to do ever since an earlier accident in America when riding his Triumph motorcycle. It was why, when on stage he stooped forward when singing.

It was when his withered leg troubled him, that he became bad tempered, sometimes giving up and hobbling off the stage,which he did on this occasion too. Tony took over the singing and the audience hardly noticed that Gene's spot had finished early. Tony Sheridan could be very professional!

Gene Vincent had always been an important figure to most of us playing rock and roll in those life-changing, radical days. As well as being one of the first and most famous of the stars to visit England, he was also unique, with a voice that sounded like no other,. Although he was a 'rocker' and wrote,'Be Bop a Lu la', he could make his songs sound really silky-smooth and honest; He also sang the most beautiful ballads. The range of his voice was incredible, as was Roy Orbison's, and sometimes Gene sounded almost female. I really loved his 'Over the Rainbow.' One of the greatest ballads I have ever heard a 'rocker' sing.

Apart from his name being in the Rock 'n' roll hall of fame, Gene Vincent's name was also in the Rockabilly hall of fame at the same time, the first singer to have had this honour.

Tony and Gene Vincent, as I have said, got on well, and had a great respect for each other, but the car accident, in which Eddie Cochrane was killed, and Gene seriously injured, had aggravated Gene's withered leg even more. Tony should have been in the car when it crashed, but Eddie Cochran had his girlfriend, Sharon Sheeley, with him as well as Gene, and there wasn't room for Tony who had to make his own way back to London by train.

Sharon Sheeley was a world renowned songwriter. She wrote songs for Eddie Cochran, as well as writing hits for Brenda Lee, Ricky Nelson and Glen Campbell. It turned out to be fortunate that Tony wasn't in the car when it crashed. It was also fortunate for us, as it was shortly after arriving back in London that he joined the 'Jets' when we badly needed a good lead guitarist to take to Germany with us, and at last I was able to meet Tony Sheridan after searching for him for so long.

After the crash Gene went back to America, and a year later his manager, Don Arden brought him back to England while we were playing at the 'Star Club'. Don asked us to back Gene Vincent once more as the previous UK tour with Gene had been a success. This time it would be an even more interesting tour to Israel: Travelling by ship from Venice to Haifa.

The 'Star Combo' was to make its own way to the 'Caliph Club'. Gene was to fly out with his nurse/girlfriend and join us there. It was September 1962. We drove across Europe and the Alps to Venice in Roy Young's Ford 'Taunus' car. It was a scary drive as we hadn't allowed ourselves enough time and were panicking a bit. Roy was driving too fast over the alpine roads. But we arrived in Venice safely, and with time to spare.

The ship was waiting, but Tony and I decided to go down to the quayside and ride on a Gondola before the ship left for Israel. Venice is beautiful, except the sea level is only inches away from flooding the whole city, which made it look like it was slowly sinking into the sea. We left on time, and the ship's first port of call was Piraeus in Greece.

Again, Tony and I, this time with Johnny Watson, went ashore to take in a bit of culture by travelling to Athens; We took a taxi to the Parthenon,(the temple of Athena) and although in ruins, it was easy to imagine what an impressive and beautiful place Athens once was. We left Greece, our heads full of wonder and respect for ancient history, and rejoined the ship. After a beautifully smooth crossing we finally arrived at the docks in Haifa, Israel.

From the ships rails we could see the extensive ribbon of white sandy beaches stretching along the coast, and in the distance was the modern city of Tel Aviv. We took a taxi to the 'Caliph Club'. It wasn't a 'posh' place by any means, in fact it was quite small and ordinary, and like most other night clubs all over the world. You can't help noticing how sterile and drab they all look in the cold light of day, and how bright and sparkly by night! Gene had arrived in Israel with his nurse/girlfriend and of course, being the main star, meant that both he and his partner had been booked into a better hotel than ours.

Tony, as always, was looking for problems, and wanted to explore the 'Caliph' to get a 'feel' of the place, but also to make sure all was well with the equipment. It turned out to be a wise thing to do. The boss, a man of few words, took us to the stage,with its barely-big-enough dance floor in front of it. There he left us to sort out our own problems, and strode moodily away.

We looked for the amplifiers and mikes, which we were told would be supplied, intending to do a test, having already been let down before at other places due to faulty equipment. This time we wouldn't trust to luck. Sure enough we were in for a shock when we saw what had been left out for us to use. There were two ancient megaphone-shaped speakers, probably left behind by Rommel in the North African desert after El Alamein, and which may have later been used by others to make public announcements, and now finally doubling up for use as speakers by visiting bands. They were old enough to be exhibited in a museum!

'What the fuck are these!' said an angry Tony, 'Where's the boss?' The owner eventually arrived back on the scene to see what all the fuss was about, but he was less than helpful.

'You said you had all the equipment!' complained Tony; 'We can't use this – it's rubbish' The boss looked agitated and very angry, and was now intent on exerting his authority.

'Well, you should have brought your own!'

responded the now livid boss, 'That's what musicians are supposed to do. Isn't it?' But Tony wouldn't let go,

'You said you had microphones and speakers at the club' said Tony speaking very slowly.

'That's it, in front of you,' shouted the angry boss, not used to being spoken to like that.

'You'll have to make do with it until I can find something better' and stormed off, severely rattled. This was his club and no interloper was going to dictate to him about what he should or shouldn't be doing. We tried the equipment out and it was as bad as we thought it would be – totally unsuitable and totally unacceptable.

Tony called the boss back and told him we couldn't use it, and therefore couldn't play.

At last the boss relented and stormed off without saying anything, and soon more modern equipment was provided. There was no way Gene

Vincent would have used this ancient stuff – remembering what happened with the microphone at Haverfordwest in Wales.

The 'Caliph club' was full of young excited Israelis on that eagerly awaited first night. They were all keen to get a look at Gene Vincent – who they had heard only on records. The fans here were no different from those in any of the other places we had played at.

But on seeing Gene some Israelis were taken aback by his strange appearance and were baffled by his aggressive black leathers, but mostly it was his bewildered-looking,wild staring eyes, which constantly looked skywards, as if looking for someone, or something else. It was not what they expected. He was greeted with silence. I suppose he really must have looked a bit weird to this new audience, which had never seen him perform.

It didn't help that he never smiled, making it difficult to tell whether or not he was glad to see the audience, who now began talking amongst themselves, clearly confused. They then began showing more interest in Tony Sheridan rather than the main star, Gene Vincent.

It was time to start and Gene carefully checked the microphone by blowing into it: he then adjusted the height of the mike stand and looked over at Tony. Then, stepping forward onto his good leg, he pulled the mike towards him, so as to take the strain off of his damaged leg. His large staring eyes were now peeping over the top of the microphone.

'Be Bop A Lula' she's my baby...'

Gene hadn't waited for us, and went straight into the song. The young audience erupted with delight and straight away began singing along with him, some rushing to the dance floor and throwing themselves around in a style that was only vaguely similar to rock 'n' roll dancing and nowhere near as good as the young Hamburgers danced in Germany.

Others were trying to get as near to the stage as possible, so as to get a better look at the famous Gene Vincent. Sometimes their eyes would scarily meet Gene's, as he looked first at them, and then fixedly upwards, over the top of the microphone and up to the sky.

I could plainly see the fans looks of curiosity, mixed with a sprinkling of awe. But Gene was as I said, not at his best – as few of us are when our heart's not in it, or we are in pain. He was still secretly drinking heavily and not eating enough, living just on his usual bottle of Vodka for breakfast.

He must have sung 'Be Bop a Lula' a thousand times, and was finding it more and more difficult to, 'sing it like he meant it'. He showed the strain of alcoholism on his pale, drawn and tortured face, where once there was only the eagerness and innocence of youth.

His act ended with quiet, polite clapping: rather than the thunderous cheers and stamping Gene had once enjoyed in his earlier days, and which now seemed to be so long ago. But most of the time he was with us, his voice was clear and soft and it never wavered. It was the dynamism and honesty that were missing.

Once again Tony would come to the rescue, whenever it was his turn to play, and as soon as he did, the whole mood of the club changed, and once again the young, happy Israeli crowd, was dancing and singing wildly, as had so often happened whenever Tony Sheridan was on stage.

From now on it was Tony, and not the main act, who would be the star attraction at the 'Caliph'.

His aggressive guitar-playing style and magnetic 'presence' were irresistible to every audience, and they were soon having a great time. They preferred Tony to Gene, as he knew which songs would get them going, and he would always put everything into it.

That was always Tony's way. He couldn't do it any differently. 'Full-on' was the only way he knew. Gene saw what was happening and was understandably not happy about it. The stage in the 'Caliph Club' was small, and Gene preferred a big stage, to give him more space and impact, but he must have known the drink was not helping his performance either, and once again it was sad to see him brought so low in his twilight years. It seems we must all eventually pay the price for our life-styles; There is no escape from it.

That first evening in Israel ended with the appearance of a dusky, overweight belly dancer, who was clearly well past her sell-by date as she writhed, wobbled and flopped, about the stage, and then into the audience, and around the tables, while making an unsuccessful attempt to appear sexy. It must have been terrible for her that people were taking absolutely no notice, despite all her efforts. Her problem was she had far too much competition with all the beautiful women in the audience, but at least she was getting paid!

Tony always attracted beautiful women to himself, wherever he appeared, and here in Israel it was no different. As soon as we had finished playing he was approached by one of them, who was accompanied by her mother, they invited Tony to their table for a drink, where the three of them spent much of the evening in deep conversation, and were to become friends.

That evening Tony and the two females left the club together. Gene had also left the club for his hotel with his girl friend/nurse. The rest of us stayed on for a while at the club before going back to our hotel, intending not to look around the town until the next day. It had been a long trip, and we were pleased just to sit down and 'chill out' for a while.

A couple of days later we were all on stage at the 'Caliph', waiting for Gene to arrive, when news came in that he was on his way to hospital; He had told someone he was dying, but on arrival at the hospital he was refused admission. The procedure In Israel at that time, was for the ambulances to be met by a doctor at the hospital entrance, whose main job was to make an assessment as to the seriousness of the case, and then make a decision as to whether or not to admit the patient. The doctor who assessed Gene, found that he was under the influence of alcohol and refused him entrance. Gene was removed from the ambulance and left by the side of the road.

Again it was pitiful to learn his career was ending in such an undignified way. His girlfriend/nurse was by his side, but could do nothing to help him. Not long after the hospital incident we learnt that Gene had made a will and left his leg-brace, made from an expensive metal, to an unknown beneficiary.

It was time for Gene to go and he returned to England: never to sing in Israel again.

The last we heard was that after Gene was back in the UK, he had joined Little Richard on tour. Tony Sheridan was now the main attraction at the 'Caliph' Club' and everyone was happy about, the place was thumping. It continued that way night after night, and we regularly played to packed houses. Before long, people came from far and wide, having   heard about Tony's talent and wanting to see him. He behaved himself well during the time we were at the 'Caliph', that is, as far as I knew!

Our afternoons and days off were spent on the beautiful white sandy beaches, the ones we had seen from the ship when we first arrived in the port at Haifa. Tony was rarely with us, spending more and more time with the Israeli girl and her mother, the ones he had met earlier at the 'Caliph'. He later told me the mother was involved with the Simon   Wiesenthal   Centre   dealing   with compensation for victims of the Holocaust.

I met them once at the club, when Tony introduced me to them. The daughter was both beautiful and intelligent and her mother was not bad either. They were the kind Tony liked to spend time with, being an intelligent guy himself, he took an interest in everyone he could learn something from, or were somehow different. He was a 'people person'.

Most women loved Tony: not only because he was good-looking and talented, but more importantly, because he listened to what they had to say (although others would contradict me and say he had a reputation for not treating women very well at all!). There was hardly any interesting subject that he didn't know at least a little about, and sometimes he knew more than I had expected.

As I have already said, Tony was secretly a spiritual person, which few people knew about. He preferred to hide it under an arrogant and uncaring façade. Why he felt a need to use this 'alter ego' I will never know. It could have been he felt he was a rock 'n roller, which didn't sit well with his spirituality – or maybe he just wanted to surprise you! I don't know, he merely 'lived it' and followed his instincts wherever they led him.

Much later, after I had returned to the UK to live, I received a letter from him which at the time would unexpectedly tell me more about Tony, his thoughts and future intentions.

It was dated 27.9.71...

"Dear old mate,

Was great to see you over here after so long. Pity there wasn't a bit more time to get together. I'll certainly visit you, when I'm next in England – maybe we can have another 'blow' together. Well, I didn't get the 'bread' from the Tennis Club gig in Flottbek – the guy came round to Calli's house next day with the law and retrieved his 'stolen' equipment! Carole and I have been round to see Calli a couple of times – he's a good face.

By the way Carole has signed a contract with Metronome, as a solo artist, and will be recording in the next two weeks – can't be bad. As for me I'm having a bit of trouble with these contractual affairs, and as yet can't record under my own name – which is a drag. However, I've just finished an LP with Drafi Deutscher. It's a sort of Les Humphries type thing, in German – the LP will be released under the group name,' WIR.' How's that?!

You never know... I've done a few shows on my own (acoustic) and have been quite successful in that field. I still get a lot of work – It seems there isn't much competition on the 'quiet' scene. Wait until I start recording again!...In the meantime I'm going to study Anglistik and Germanistik at Hamburg University, well, I've got the time and inclination. Otherwise I'm not too sure about the future. 'Spose I'm a Gypsy at heart 'Die wanderlust hat mich wieder gepackt! (The desire to wander has gripped me again!) Horst (Fascher) and I are planning to do a tour of Japan sometime next year. You know, with a band, with his wife and Carole singing as well. Horst has really changed – Vietnam had a hand in that, and of course the fact that he doesn't drink to excess anymore – he smokes! By the way Carole and I are getting married soon. If you could be here, there's nobody else I can think of who I'd rather have as a best man. We can't really wait until you're over here again! So next time we see you, I'll be hitched (again) for the last time. You know, Colin, I've often thought seriously about doing something completely different – something absolutely nutty like the army or even the police or customs – but every time I'm on that stage, letting off steam, and the crowd's there with me, I'm in my element. It must be in my blood or something. In a way I envy you, but then again a man's gotta be free....Oh yeahh. How's the force treating you constable? Great, I hope. How is the wife/ kids? Fine? Great. Write if you have time, and let me know what's going on in sunny Southampton. I'd appreciate it. Hope you're all well,

God Bless... Your old comrade – Tony"

Tony really was a 'chancer',and the Tennis club he referred to in his letter was the swanky Hamburg Tennis Club. A 'gig' which Tony managed to turn into a riot. As a result the angry boss had refused to pay us at the end of the evening, and we decided we would take their amplifiers and equipment until he did, which was why the boss had called the police.

Tony would deliberately tread the problem

path, where others would try to find a smoother way. He always needed to 'try it on' and experience the thrill of not knowing what would happen, or where whatever it was he was doing, might lead him. In the end, his recklessness destroyed him. It was only those who loved him, who had prevented it happening sooner.

But if Tony could choose to live his life again, I don't believe he would change a thing – although he told me (in the above letter,) that he had seriously thought about, 'doing 'something completely different, something absolutely 'nutty'.But I don't think it would have worked. Tony belonged on the stage, that is what he was best at doing, and that is what made him happy. Anything else requiring order and responsibility was out of the question.

Meanwhile, back at the 'Caliph' things became

mundane and more routine. We were expecting to get a message from Gene Vincent's agent Don Arden, telling us when Gene would be back, but we hadn't heard from him, and we knew Gene would not be returning.

But the club continued to do well, and we were happy there. We still made our own entertainment during the day, mostly centred around the beach. I also arranged for Tony, Johnny Watson and me, to fly to Jerusalem. The flight was to be in an old wartime American, 'Dakota' (a troop-carrying aircraft), which had still retained its original, battered, and well-worn seats.

It was a budget flight as you can guess! Costing the equivalent of five pounds per person, which was pretty cheap. We boarded the 'Dakota' at a small local airport, and as soon as we were all seated the engines spluttered and banged, before roaring into life. We careered slowly down the potholed runway, lifting a few feet off the ground and then coming back down again. The aircraft wasn't overloaded, as there were only five of us on board!.

The old girl just didn't want to leave the safety of the airport, and seemed to be telling us so. Eventually, with just a few yards of runway left, she decided she would take off after all, and rattled and shook her way up into the sky. The view over this ancient land was stunning, and history was visible with every ruin that passed beneath us. The scenes alone were worth the £5 flight. But every now and again the old Dakota wobbled a little, then shook all over, veering from left to right and I predicted a scary landing, when, or if, we ever got to where we were going.

Thankfully we were able to see our destination, an old airport, just like the one we had left behind, and in the distance the domes of Jerusalem. I wasn't sorry to be getting off the old girl, and looked forward to wandering around the streets of Jerusalem, but first we had to land. Tony took it all in his stride, completely not phased by any thoughts of danger.

The Dakota rushed towards the runway veering again from left to right. I pictured the pilot wrestling with the controls. There was a violent bump as the wheels hit the runway and the aircraft bounced off to one side: the old girl wasn't even able to travel in a straight line!

It was like one of those scary, 'white knuckle' theme-park rides, as we tightly gripped our seats. Thankfully the plane did stop, quite scarily, and only just before running out of runway again. We clapped our hands in appreciation of the pilot, but also in relief, and pictured him sitting in the cockpit, pale-faced and making the sign of the cross, while shaking all over. We left the aircraft and boarded a mini-bus which had come to meet us, and take us to Jerusalem and the 'Church of the Holy Sepulchre'. There was a deathly hush as we entered the holy place where Jesus had lain, it was an atmosphere we could all feel.

Tony was transfixed and unusually quiet. I could tell by his wide-eyed look, that he was moved by this place. Then he did something shocking, which I should have expected. He reached up to the low rocky ceiling of the tomb and tried to pick off a piece of rock from the low roof, possibly as a souvenir. With Tony you never knew what was coming next!

'Stop it Tony', said Johnny Watson abruptly, and Tony did as he was told. Sometimes it's little mental snapshots like this that we remember – Tony about to desecrate the tomb, and Johnny Watson (not a churchgoer) unexpectedly trying to stop him.

We returned safely – in time for the evening session at the 'Caliph'. It had been a strange, moving day in Jerusalem, but I was glad we went there. I was also glad Johnny Watson of all people, wanted to go with us, having never showed any interest in such things before. Maybe he just wanted to come along for the ride, or maybe we didn't really know him.

Who knows what goes on in the minds of the people we think we know well? I'm not an expert on such things. Others who don't know me, would have been just as puzzled to see me, a rock 'n' roller, secretly entering St Josephs Catholic church opposite the 'Kaiser Keller' to talk to someone I couldn't see!

Neither Tony nor Johnny ever talked about the Jerusalem visit again, maybe in both their minds it really did clash with rock 'n' roll, which seems a silly notion to me now.

But I knew that Tony, after being brought up a Catholic, now followed his own spiritual pathway to enlightenment, and a search for a pathway to his God.

Tony believed the Buddha was the way. We had argued about the existence of a 'Supreme Being' but never got anywhere. It is an idea that not even Science will investigate, despite the evidence of countless witnesses down the centuries. Religion and Theology are avoided by Science at all costs, which seems strange to me. Knowledge is knowledge no matter what kind it is Even the noble science of Natural Theology is no more, and the religious beliefs of those great scientific giants, Isaac Newton and Charles Darwin (who did believe in a god) are taboo subjects as far as Science is concerned, and never discussed or investigated in any scientific way. This, despite there being no human tribe on Earth, no matter how cut off or remote, that does not believe in some form of a 'Supreme Being'.

The fans at the 'Caliph' club had now taken Tony fully to their hearts, and the grumpy boss was now beaming every night as the cash flowed in. He even began bringing his own important guests and friends along, to show them how well his club was doing.

Meanwhile Don Arden, Gene Vincent's manager, had, at last been in touch, having arranged an open air rock concert for the following week in Jerusalem. He also confirmed that Gene Vincent definitely wasn't coming back to join us at the 'Caliph', nor will he be appearing at the open air concert in Jerusalem..

We arrived at the open air venue to be greeted by a huge enthusiastic crowd gathered to hear us, and were told we were the first British rock 'n' roll band to play in Israel.

But to be performing in Jerusalem made me feel uneasy. If the event had been in a 'proper' concert hall and not the open air, I would have felt much better. Tony wasn't bothered either way, and of course I went along with it. At that time bands always followed their manager's instructions – we ignored them at our peril (if we wanted more work!).

If Don Arden booked us to play in the Jerusalem streets, then that is where we will play.

Tony climbed on stage to the cheers of a large young crowd, which soon became silent again while Tony went through his usual ritual of ignoring them while he tuned his guitar.

When he had finished he gave us a nod and once again let loose with his violent and emotive guitar on the unsuspecting audience; It was a roar of primitive sound and rhythm, and then his voice.

'Come along a baby, whole lotta Shakin going on...' and the crowd was hooked – singing, dancing and shouting in one great swaying mass. It still seemed strange for me to be doing this in Jerusalem. For Tony it seemed to be quite normal and all in a day's work.

8. TIME TO GO

The contract in Israel was coming to and end. It was early October 1962 and the day of my wedding was very near. I took a flight from Tel Aviv back to Hamburg and arrived at Ingrid's home, where everyone was frantically getting things ready for the big day.

The paperwork, including my baptismal certificate, had arrived from England at last. But the old-school German priest, in his pre-marriage guidance talk, told us he was against the wedding, and would have to clear permission for it with the Bishop.

Ingrid was a protestant and I was a Catholic. He predicted that even if it is allowed, our marriage wouldn't last, and during an informal discussion afterwards, he said that men would never land on the moon. He was not exactly a bundle of fun, and he was wrong in both his predictions (the Americans did land on the moon, and I'm still married to Ingrid!).

But what really upset Ingrid and I, more than anything else, was that we arrived at the church to find out, without any previous warning, that our wedding was to be a double one. Another couple had arrived on the same day to be married in the same church, and at the same time as us, and thereby completely spoiling our big day!

The other marriage was also between a couple of mixed religions (a mixed marriage) they, too, must have been extremely upset. Neither of us had any idea that this was going to happen until it was too late! Otherwise I would have gone to another church. Any church!

It was all a long time ago, but the memories of that sad day still hurt. I talked to Tony about it, and of course he couldn't help. It was a difficult one, as the deed had already been done.

I also shared my thoughts with Tony about my becoming more and more disillusioned with Germany, and of returning to England. Firstly there was my troubled experiences in the workplace alongside the Germans, and now the church wedding. I had originally planned to stay in Germany with Ingrid, but I now had serious doubts that it could ever work, and had decided that Ingrid and I will be better off by moving to England and setting up home there.

I also told Tony about the time I was walking

home from work one evening in central Hamburg, and was reprimanded by the police for walking on the grass, even though there were no signs telling me not to do it. I felt there were too many minor laws in Germany, a lot more than in England, and I began to feel restricted – like wearing a straight-jacket.

This may sound a bit trivial to you, the reader, but together with the other problems I had experienced, it meant I would always have the feeling of being trapped, if I stayed in Germany much longer. Tony listened intently, then said quietly, and sincerely,

'I would rather you stayed here, Colin, but you must do what you think is right. But whatever you decide to do, we must keep in touch.' I assured him we would. He looked upset, but didn't try to persuade me not to go, and I went with my instincts, which told me I must leave Germany if there was to be any chance of my starting a new life and career.

From then on my sole focus was on England and Ingrid; I would go as soon as I had finished my time with the band. Others had made up my mind for me .Johnny had made it easy for me, as I only needed to contact him in Southampton and he will arrange somewhere for Ingrid and me to stay. I could now plan my move.

I contacted Johnny and told him what I intended to do. Johnny told me I had made the right decision, Southampton was a great city and there was no problem; He would do what I asked and I was not to worry about where to stay. I only needed to tell him when Ingrid and I were coming.

Don't get me wrong, I don't dislike the Germans, there are some wonderful people there, (as there are everywhere in the world!), but I needed to feel secure. I was now married, and looking to the future: which meant making a new life away from rock 'n' roll.

That new life could only be in England. What kind of job I would take up would be decided when I arrived there. Meanwhile I would stay with the band at the 'Star Club'.

But Tony Sheridan's talent can never be be ignored for long and sure enough while playing at the 'Star Club' we received great news! ...

9. CHUBBY CHECKER

Tony Sheridan and the 'Beat Brothers' (the 'Jets' name had changed again!) were to join the huge 'Chubby Checker' European tour with dozens of other artists. It would delay my return to England but it didn't matter. Again we were playing for Don Arden (Gene Vincent's agent), but Gene wouldn't be coming with us and we weren't given a reason why.

The artists on the tour were mostly American, British, German and many other stars from lesser known regions of Europe. We knew many of them, and all of them had heard of Tony Sheridan. It was an enormous tour, visiting twenty-three major European cities in Austria, Germany, and Switzerland. It was at a time when Chubby Checker was at his most popular, and was much loved wherever he went. He was a great showman and a great guy.

It was to be the biggest professional tour we had been invited to take part in. It would start in Basel, Switzerland, and end in Berlin. It was hectic, and extremely tiring on our twelve day schedule – but, at the same time we were well looked after, and made many new friends. The whole thing was something quite special and not to be forgotten!

Apart from Chubby Checker, the main star, there was a mixture of American stars including Jack Hammer: a talented singer, dancer, and songwriter, as well as one of the early members of the 'Platters'. He had written many of their great hit songs, as well as 'Great Balls of Fire': which was made famous by Jerry Lee Lewis.

Also on tour with us was an all American girl band, 'Goldie and the Gingerbreads' one of the first all female rock bands to play at the famous

'Peppermint Lounge' in New York. Their band was made up of Nancy, Margo, Ginger and Goldie. Tony was to get to know them well. They were all great musicians and later on in their careers crossed over to playing jazz rather than rock music.

Tony got to know all the artists on the tour, including Paul Wurges, a very good German guitarist. It was he who formed the first German Rock and roll band. Also on the tour, was singer, Billy Sanders,who had great success in Germany. He was an English boy from a coal-mining family in the north of England, who later joined the army as a guardsman, serving at Buckingham Palace!

The mixture of talent was quite varied, with singer, 'Nora Nova' a Bulgarian, who had made it big in Germany, she sang not only jazz, but also some of the beautiful classics.

Also touring with us was 'Manuela', an

attractive German pop singer. She had a big hit with 'Schuld war nur der Bossa Nova' (It was only the fault of the 'Bossa Nova').

Also on the bill was another American – an ex GI named Mal Sondock, who became an actor, singer and TV star, based in Germany. Finally there was 'Ambros Seelos' and his famous international show orchestra: giving the whole tour even greater variety.

We travelled together in coaches and soon got to know each other: each of us interested in the other's act. I couldn't help noticing how well behaved Tony was on this particular tour, and wondered if it was because he was under the direction of Don Arden. If only Don Arden had managed Tony earlier! But as already said, Don Arden had no intention of doing so.

He had already seen and heard how

troublesome Tony was, and up until now, had only used Tony as a backing guitarist/singer. He had refused to sign him up permanently – even though he had long recognized Tony's talent.

One of the enduring memories of the 'Chubby Checker' tour, apart from the wonderful camaraderie among the artists, was the memory of our band, the 'Beat Brothers': Appearing as mere pinpricks on the enormous stage in the Vienna State Hall – our tiny band of four, looking abandoned, alone and forlorn, swallowed up in the middle of the vast football-pitch sized, classical stage, designed for full-scale orchestras and ballet productions.

We were made to look insignificant, with wide unused areas of the stage on each side of us, and the whole of it surrounded by an audience of 20,000 people. But Tony was at his best that night, and we went down exceptionally well. It ended with thunderous applause from the huge audience. And after an extremely successful tour, Tony and the 'Beat Brothers' returned to the 'Star Club' to play once more as the 'Star Combo' playing their own sets, as well backing visiting artists..

10. TONY SHERIDAN'S FINAL YEARS

'The Beatles' were now famous worldwide, and had returned to play at the 'Star Club'. It was one of those historic moments, when the original 'Jets' (now the 'Star Combo' again) and 'The Beatles', had come full circle, and were meeting up again. The difference was, our band had stayed still and 'The Beatles' had moved on, but it could have been so different. 'The Beatles' were happy to meet up with Tony again and the 'Star Combo' were pleased at 'The Beatles' worldwide success.

My last gig, before finally returning to England was at the 'Acadia' Club in Frankfurt. It was with Tony Sheridan, and featured a talented Irish boy, Jimmy Doyle, on drums. He had taken over from Johnny Watson, after Johnny had returned home to the UK to take over the running of a go-kart track at Lord Montague's motor museum in southern England's New Forest. Ricky Barnes was on sax, and myself on bass guitar.

The 'Acadia'.club was owned by two Jewish gentlemen, and visited mainly by American forces personnel, whose base was nearby. They loved Tony from the first time we played there, and were genuinely astounded that he wasn't yet a world star. The popular 'Acadia' was filled to breaking point most nights.

We were also honoured when invited to play inside the American army base, where we treated like royalty. At the end of a wild evening we were given a 'chitty' allowing us to visit the PX (Stores) and choose anything we wanted: drink, clothes, perfume etc. But there was nothing we wanted, we were just pleased they had enjoyed the music (or we were too drunk to take advantage of the offer, I can't remember!).

I lost count of the number of times various

Americans had urged Tony to go to America, where he would be guaranteed to be smash hit, but he always brushed off these ideas, as he had done on many other occasions during his career. It was a long-standing mystery.

Looking back, Tony's biggest mistake, without a doubt, was to turn down the offer by Brian Epstein to return to England with The Beatles', and continue working with them as he had done in Germany. He inexplicably refused this once in a lifetime chance.

He should also have seriously considered other offers made before and after that, such as when the American stars, Joey Dee and the 'Starliters' offered to take Tony to New York and introduce him to the famous 'Peppermint Lounge' in New York, where Joey would sponsor Tony and make him known throughout America.

Joey Dee and the 'Starliters' were once the

house band at the 'Peppermint Lounge' and had made a number of hit records, which were recorded 'live' there. They were still enormous stars in America and Tony would have benefited greatly from their support.

As pointed out earlier, Tony showed no interest, and deliberately shunned success and no one but he knew the reason why he should turn his back on so many opportunities, and then make it worse by ruining much of the considerable success he had gained so far.

In answer to my questions put to him about his unacceptable behaviour, and refusal to move on and progress, all he would say was what he had said before, 'That's me Colin, I'm Tony Sheridan – the loose cannon!' That was all I ever got from him; He had no plan in place. He lived for today and let tomorrow take care of itself.

Then, one terrible evening on 22nd November 1963, while we were on stage playing at the 'Acadia' in Frankfurt, we heard the tragic news that president Kennedy had been shot. We were all stunned, as was the whole of Germany and the world. Evil finds a way to kill its enemies. It was soon after the assassination that the 'Acadia' 'gig' came to an end, and Tony was called back to Hamburg. There was more work for him to do at Polydor.

My own life was also about to change completely – very soon I will be returning to England. Sadly there was no chance to say goodbye to 'My old mate' Tony Sheridan before I left Germany – everything had been done in a rush. The plan was for Ingrid to stay behind until I had found a job and then I would send for her.

I arrived in Southampton and settled quickly in

at Johnny Watson's family Guest House in the centre of Southampton, and while there I looked for work. In the meantime I joined Johnny Watson's band with Tex Roberg as main singer. There was always plenty of work in Southampton.

We played at pubs and clubs in Southampton which allowed me to earn a small amount of money until I found a 'proper' job, I started as a furniture salesman and then joined the Police in Southampton, which was more interesting, more exciting and more worthwhile.

It wasn't long before I was chosen to be a detective in the Criminal investigation Department (CID). But all this time I was still playing in a Southampton band up until a message came from the Chief Constable ordering me to stop playing in what he thought were 'sleazy night clubs', as it wasn't compatible with my job as a policeman!. Tony asked me if I could get him into the police, but I knew it wouldn't be possible, and I didn't try.

He and I kept in touch until the end, mainly by letter, but also by visiting him when I was in Germany. He also came to see me in Southampton, and we played together again at the 'Top Rank', a popular dance hall in the city. It was a bit of a disaster as Tony started trouble again, by going up on stage up and telling the lead guitarist to hand over his guitar, as he, Tony Sheridan, wanted to play. At first I didn't know what had happened, as I was in the audience talking to Johnny Watson.

Then I saw Tony calling me up on stage to join him. Luckily some of the band knew who Tony was, but didn't like his arrogant manners. Understandably the lead guitarist was angry at being approached in the way Tony had done, but Tony was immune to resentment.

Once on stage, he also demanded the bass guitarist give up his bass so that I could play too. We started, and Tony subsequently 'brought the house down', doing several Jerry Lee Lewis numbers. Everyone was asking who he was (he had never played in Southampton before). We did a few extra numbers and the crowd went wild – They loved him!

'Who is he?' 'Who is he?' excited fans were asking me afterwards. The band was now much happier and thought it was worthwhile letting Tony Sheridan play – even though, at first, they were not happy about him using their instruments and being so aggressive.

I was to return to Germany and make several visits to Tony's home in Seestermuehe at the invitation of Tony and his beautiful wife, Anna. I also went back to Hamburg to play, accompanying Tony on various smaller gigs in and around Hamburg.

It was always good to see him again. We went back a long way, and whenever we met it was a great occasion, with lots of back-slapping and leg-pulling by two happy mates.

There was one last, great occasion to come, when: Tony, Roy Young, Ricky Barnes, Jimmy Doyle and I came together to play as the 'Star Combo' in a Hamburg reunion.

The event was held at the 'Fliegende Bauten' A music theatre close to the top end of the Reeperbahn. It was to commemorate the 50th Anniversary of the opening of the 'Star Club' in 1962 and was organized by King Size (Ted) Taylor from Liverpool. It was King Size who rescued Tony's beautiful 'Martin' Guitar – the one Tony had when we first arrived in Hamburg with the 'Jets', and which Tony later smashed up on stage. Ted did a deal with Tony and had the 'Martin' restored. The deal was for Tony to get a cash adjustment and King Size's Gibson 335 guitar as part of the deal This likeable giant (King Size) will always be remembered by me and many others. I see him now on stage at the 'Star Club' in his huge check sports jacket and singing, 'Don't know much about history... don't know much about..'

The 50th anniversary event was to be held over two days, as there were so many bands and singers wanting to take part. And there were lots of tales, and exaggerated stories to tell each other. It was even more emotional to be playing once more with Tony, Roy Young, Jimmy Doyle, and Ricky Barnes – reliving many great memories of our experiences in Hamburg. We would never forget those early days when we first arrived, not knowing what to expect.

It was around this time, or a bit earlier, that I noticed a dramatic change in Tony's whole personality and demeanour. It seemed to come from within. He became a totally different person from the wild boy of yesteryear, the boy who had caused so much heartache to those who loved him – although most of these caring people never abandoned him.

Now in his final years, Tony became a much gentler person, much more concerned about others, whereas before, he didn't give a toss about anybody he didn't feel close to.

It was because I had known him for so long (since the early 2'i's days in London) that this sudden softening, and dramatic change in him, had become more noticeable to me, and was possibly missed by others.

I remembered him saying in a letter how determined he was to change direction, and

I don't know if this new attitude had anything to do with his mounting illnesses, or some other significant event. He became more and more involved in doing music related good works such as the Hamburg TV workshops, demonstrating 60's music to children, concerts for prison inmates and drug offenders, as well as shows for church organisations, schools and universities. They were part of a huge list of works accomplished by Tony Sheridan, before his busy life came to an end.

From a young age he had always pushed himself relentlessly – now older he continued to add to it, with more music trips worldwide, often to places with unpronounceable names, and usually working as a solo artist, pushing and testing his stamina to an extent which would cripple others half his age. He had loads of energy, which had been visible ever since he first started to play guitar and sing. No one can confine that much energy. It must be released or it explodes – which explains why he sometimes did exactly that – explode.

Alongside this new, milder attitude, I noticed a certain frailty about him too, a kind of weakness creeping into his voice, and at times he looked terribly old and tired. Like Gene Vincent before him, he was ageing fast, but Tony was still determined to keep up the pace and it wasn't good to watch it happening.

He had no intention of retiring yet, and was like a candle left to burn to the very end – until its wick begins to flicker and struggle – eventually burning itself out. It was as if he wanted to give the world everything he had, but there was little left to give, only pieces of himself.

Even so, right to the end, Tony was able to show he was still the master guitarist, singer and showman, and the same talented musician I had known since we were young.

Despite everything, and with all his many problems, he insisted on working to the end.

However, his body was unable to stand the merciless pace he continually demanded of it, and although physically strong, there is a limit as to what was achievable.

He was taken ill in Italy and brought back to Germany where he died,on 17th February 2013.

It was a great shock to most, but to me, although devastating, it was not unexpected.

I was at Tony's well-attended funeral service in the 'Michels Kirche' in Hamburg, close to the Reeperbahn and St Pauli, where we first played together in Germany. There a German friend of Tony gave a wonderful and fitting oration. There was a genuine sense of loss felt by the many people present. The 'Michels Kirche is a huge church – more like a Cathedral.

It is a place where funeral services for people of note and merit are held, and amongst others, included Helmut Schmidt, former Chancellor of West Germany, and a great Hamburg statesman.

It was therefore a great honour for Tony's family, that his funeral service was held in such a special place, as Tony was neither German nor a public figure, but he was a great artist.

It was also an honour for me, too, when members of Tony's family asked me to give the funeral speech in English – which of course I agreed to do, thinking it would be easy. But it wasn't. Parts of my recollections made it too difficult to keep control and to hold back my own emotions.

Since a young child I had always been told by my parents, that girls may cry, but not boys. But inwardly, during the funeral oration, I was distraught, as were most of us in attendance at the ceremony. Especially Tony's German and English families, and his many fans present on that sad day. Deep down he was loved by all those who knew him well. Some loved him just for the joy his music gave them – others just loved him – many tears were shed that mournful day, and those who didn't love him were forced to respect his talent

. Few people, even those who knew him well, had any idea what Tony planned to do when he could no longer play, or no longer wished to play.

From his letters he told me what his intentions were. He had already said he was going to 'change himself'. I knew he didn't only mean a new career. He meant to change his inner self, as well as to seek new worldly challenges in art and especially,

'Heraldry'. He succeeded in both before he died and told me about them in his letters.

I don't know how he came to be so heavily involved in the Heraldic Art scene, but he did send me my own Irish family's coat of arms, beautifully hand-painted on parchment in rich colours. Tony told me in another letter that he had been admitted as a 'Craft Member' to the 'Society of Heraldic Arts' ,and the piece of work he had submitted to the Society for judgement of his suitability to be accepted into the Heraldic Society, was the same one he had painted for me and featured my original family name, Crowley.

At the same time he planned to return to Art college to obtain a diploma, which would help him in his new career in Heraldry. He must have known it would be difficult, and few would take him seriously. But I knew him better. He was a strong and determined person;

If he focussed his mind on achieving something, my money was on him achieving it.

The only problem he had, which was not a small one, was to erase his earlier reputation as a talented, but wild boy, someone who couldn't be relied on. It was a reputation that had followed him to Germany, and was reinforced there, due to his well-known bad behaviour.

He was widely known in England as an 'untouchable' among managers and agents; Don Arden had used Tony before, as I have said, but even he wouldn't take him on permanently saying, 'I could never find him when I needed him'. Jack Good had sacked Tony from his BBC shows, right at the beginning of Tony's music career, and Tony's reputation had spread.

This meant few well respected managers were prepared to risk taking him under their wing: they had their reputations to think of, and even if any of them did risk it, they rarely went back for more. His saving grace was always his wonderful talent which, as I said, meant he always had work. Not necessarily huge 'gigs' like the Chubby Checker tour, although he had those, too, but usually much smaller ones, which he preferred.

In fact Tony had enough work to keep him continually occupied. Much of his later career was collaborating with other high profile artists at home and abroad, and apart from working with 'The Beatles' he worked with: Roy Young, Gerry Marsden – who Tony said stole 'You'll Never Walk Alone' from his repertoire, not that Tony was worried about it!,

He also worked with the great guitarist Albert Lee in Italy with whom he made an LP (Dawn Colours) featuring the La Scala Orchestra of Milan.

He dedicated the 'Dawn Colours' album to John, Paul, George and Ringo. He also worked with other talented British and German artists such as Drefi Deutscher, with whom Tony had also made an LP.

He was now back composing his own music, and told me in a letter (dated 31st April 1994) how he was *"busy getting some music together to send to Paul McCartney as he, (Paul) would like to hear some "new sounds" "please say a prayer for me on this issue – It all helps!"*ending it with, *"Blessings galore to you all, Love TS."*

But the older mature Tony wanted to do more – to reach out and teach music, which he had previously done in Norfolk, starting many years earlier as leader of the sixth form school orchestra and later with his many backing bands, including The Beatles'.

He told me more about these things in another of his letters date 9th March 1994, and how, in later life, he sought to make a contribution to peace and culture. I can see some of you smiling – I didn't smile, as I knew Tony was deadly serious about it. He had changed his priorities in life quite dramatically.

He was, as I said earlier, a changed character, far quieter and more tolerant now, and actively seeking my support to sponsor him for entry into a papal order of chivalry, (the 'Order of St Sylvester') by writing to the Bishop of Hamburg, Dr Hans-Jochen Jaschke, recommending Tony's admission into the order. Tony wrote...

"I admit it all sounds a trifle high-faluting" *"But essentially St Sylvester' comprises of artists & musicians etc. who share a mutual interest in things chivalric. Members do not even have to be Catholics (although by baptism I am) Your own*

parish priest could also apply to the Bishop in question. Please do as you see fit – any assistance is appreciated."

It seemed a strange thing to ask me to do. But I did make some enquiries on Tony's behalf but they were unsuccessful. There were strict guidelines which Tony also mentions in his letter... *"The lay person may submit anyone's name for admittance (to the Order of St Sylvester) provided the candidate in question has contributed in some real measure to the arts, and consequently to the cause of peace amongst all mankind"* Tony goes on to write, *"Certainly, our efforts have resulted in much reaping from a few seeds planted in Hamburg – music has done much & continues to be a force for good in this crazy old world, (God bless us, me ole mate"!)* He then writes, *"Please let me know if you agree to this slightly vain proposal"* The letter moved on to ask how my fireplace-making business was getting on: one of them had been entered at the National Woodworker show in London, and had won a gold medal. Tony was quite impressed!

"How are your fireplaces etc going down in the old country? I do hope your work gives you a lot of satisfaction as a creative outlet, and that one day, possibly, you will grace my future hearth with a result of your capable hands. Of course, I hope to be in the position to pay you a preposterously high price for a suitable 'custom job! We both may have to wait a couple of years more, but the day is hazily in sight, just over the horizon." He continues,

"Roy Young phoned me a few weeks ago with an amazing proposition. Calling from Miami he asked if I were interested in joining a group called the '5th Beatles' consisting of musicians who, at some time in their careers, have played with the

Beatles. At present, Klaus Voorman, Howie Casey & Pete Best have been approached, & of course, Roy himself. Apparently the backing is financially sound, & envisages a mutual album and a US. and European tour to promote it. This all came as a slight shock – especially as I (Tony) had thought Roy to be departed from this world! (as reported from several sources). Well, I've said yes to this one, hoping we all come up with some fresh & convincing music to spread some good vibes in the World, & maybe even make a few bob in the process! I'll keep you posted... And if that is not enough – wait for it – a chap phoned from London, trying to trace ex – '2 'i's' faces for a recording venture!! This one would naturally include yourself, old mate – and Roy! We shall see – again I'll keep you in the picture as to any further developments. Life is full of surprises, that's for sure.

*I do hope the Guild (*Tony refers to a craft guild I had set up in England) *will take off successfully, if belatedly – the idea is great: craft instead of commercialism!*

"My very best of wishes to you all, & especially to Ingrid and yourself. May blessings rain upon you (as the Bishop said to the publican....."

Love Tony S.

In a later letter, dated 31ˢᵗ April 1994 (the same one in which he mentions writing music for Paul McCartney), Tony again brings up the 'St Sylvester' matter' saying,

"I feel it is important to stress the importance of our efforts in relation to the 'reconciliation achieved' by the young music of our day. In this sense it was a period of 'forgiving in action' as I'm sure you will agree. I see that we were privileged

to implement God's work". He continued with his deep message. "Without blowing the old trumpet the DDR (East Germany) tours spread not a little happiness (I hope) too. Vietnam gave a little comfort to many young, unwillingly caught up in that shameful mess. As you know, in Hamburg we inspired many young Germans to get involved in music – viz, to bridge the gap in their culture, as far as it was possible 'nough said", (Tony then changes the subject)

"How is your Guild-Project progressing? It sounds like it it could develop into a time-consuming venture, especially at the beginning. In any case, I wish you enthusiasm, & the energy to get things off the ground, as you would wish them to happen".He then goes on to say, "Have you heard about the film: 'Back Beat'? Do see it when the opportunity arises! In a sense it's about us, too. "

Blessings galore to you all

Love TS

P.S. "A chap phoned me from London, asking if I were interested in participating in an album production of ex – 2'i's' musicians. Shall keep you posted"...

This was the new Tony, that up until now had stayed hidden. He was allowing deeper, more caring thoughts to surface, and he acted on them. I suspect he knew that time was running out, and we were all getting older. It was as if he firmly intended to put everything right in his final years, and only God knows if he was successful. (I'm certain he was).

There was to be a last adventurous, and creative burst of activity before Tony was to get his 'tap on the shoulder', telling him it was time to go. After tours of Australia, France, Italy, Israel, Finland, Switzerland and the former Czechoslovakia, in and around 1966, he told me in a letter of his thirst for adventure in far-away lands. Between 1967 and 1969 he accepted a two month assignment in Vietnam, entertaining U.S. troops in the field. The two months became sixteen months and he went through the 'hottest' period of the Vietnam war (his own description). Tony was made an Honorary Captain in the U.S. Army, and for some reason the English music press reported him killed!

After Vietnam in 1969 Tony went to Sydney, Australia to recuperate. There he collaborated, recorded, toured and founded a music scene, together with other musicians, in Sydney. Then – between 1969 and 1971 he was back in Germany again to do creative work with German musicians resulting in a new gathering, known as the, "Eppendorf Scene".

Between 1972 and 1974 Tony accepted a freelance position at North German Radio (NDR Hamburg) initiating and moderating the first radio series concerned solely with black American music.

He gets a massive, positive reaction, from East German listeners and continued the series at BBC/London on a reciprocal basis – he sent me a letter with details of the things he was doing and had done, both professional and charitable.

In 1975 Tony returned to England for concerts, featuring his own music. He held a sold-out concert at the Philharmonic Hall in Liverpool, accompanied entirely by the Royal Liverpool Philharmonic Orchestra, and filmed by BBC-TV, with narration by actor, Jack Hedley. Then between 1975 and 1977, Tony made diverse recordings and TV appearances In Hamburg and also in Landskrona (Sweden) with the accent on acoustic music, which he had always loved. In 1978 Tony moved to Los Angeles for extensive recording work, staying until 1979.

In 1980 Tony returned to Hamburg.(which he now called 'home') where he continued recording and making public appearances, before going on tour again in Israel.

Still busy, between 1981 and 1983 he held various concerts in the U.S.A. and during this period and up until 1983 he was in a Berlin-workshop at Radio Rias-Berlin with Alexis Korner founder and father of the British Blues movement, and earlier part of the 'skiffle' era in the Soho cellar clubs of London. Together they featured songs of a spiritual nature.

In 1984 until 1985, probably, worn out, he sought seclusion in Denmark, but was soon working on new music. He toured Sweden, Norway and Finland, bringing experimental music in diverse formations. During this same period, Tony moved to Wuppertal, a beautiful part of Germany: hoping to find an oasis of peace for himself and his family.

He then made a journey to India, seeking the spiritual consolation he so badly needed.

During this time he is awarded a gold album by the music industry and between 1986 and 1987 Tony visited the great guitarist, Albert Lee in Milan, and together they produced a new album 'Dawn Colours' with members of the "Scala"orchestra and dedicated it to 'The Beatles' which I mentioned earlier.

He returned to Germany and during this period toured the German Democratic Republic (East Germany) up until German re-unification. In that same year he returned to Hamburg to host a TV workshop, demonstrating 60's music to children, which I have also also referred to previously.

Between 1988 and 1990 Tony was on tour, making appearances in Barcelona, Paris, New York and the Faro Islands. He also made further recordings in Denmark and a move to a house the country in northern Germany.

According to the information he sent to me, between 1991 and 1993 he made appearances in Canada and the U.S.A. bringing experimental, 'New Age' music to his audiences there.

Tony's punishing schedule continued. He told me he he provided interviews for various German radio and TV stations: WDR, ARD Cologne, Radio Bremen T.V, and DDR-T.V in Rostock

(German Democratic Republic).

Altogether it was a tremendous amount of work, both physically and mentally. It was as if Tony was determined to get as much done as he could – while it was still possible.

It clearly allows us to see how dramatically Tony's priorities had changed during the final years of his life. At last it was not all about pleasing himself and ignoring everyone else: instead it was an opportunity to put back much of what he had taken from his long association with music, and then to add more of his own newly-revealed unknown and astonishing talents which he had so far withheld, and do all this before he died.

EPILOGUE

This is the end of my story – a tale about the mysterious Anglo-Irish boy from Norfolk, England. Who he was, or who he thought he was,we shall never know, as he is no longer with us, and even when he was here, he gave no self assessment, except through his music.

All I can say is that he was a character full of contradictions and my unlikeliest friend.

He was unique – the kind of person who can never be replaced. Once he was born the mould was broken and could never be put back together again in the same way.

All Tony Sheridan had told me about himself, was that he was a 'loose cannon'. It is an old sea-going term meaning a person likened to an out-of-control cannon, which has broken loose, and is careering around the open deck of a warship in bad weather, crashing into things and damaging them – unable to be restrained or tied down. Nor could it be controlled in any way without risk of damage, or harm, to whoever tries to do so.

I will have to accept that this is how Tony saw himself when he was young and wild – except to add he was much more than that. He was also a gifted human being and a deeply caring person, which he would often hide. There is no question about his impact, as a long term mentor to the 'Beatles'; He gladly shared his talent with them, but also with others, too.

He never complained about anything, or asked for any great reward. Fame didn't impress him; His was a straight and stony path without a destination. It was an honour that he saw me as his friend, and of course I will never forget him, nor will I ever want to do so.

It is hard to tell what Tony Sheridan would

have done to keep himself occupied after he could no longer play, or no longer wanted to play; He had already given us everything.

I sincerely believe it would somehow have been connected with teaching. But one night I saw him 'through a glass darkly' in a dream; He looked up at me with his usual cheeky and mischievous smile and tilted his head to one side in questioning way,

'I bet you didn't expect me to be doing this, did you, Colin?' But I couldn't see what it was he was doing as he turned his head slowly away and was gone. Something told me that what it was, had nothing to do with teaching. He seemed to be in a better place, and if our beliefs are true, and they contradict the pessimism and limitations of proud Science, then he and I shall certainly meet again.

COLIN CRAWLEY

ABOUT THE AUTHOR

Colin Crawley born 14th April 1940 in the docklands of London, close to Tower Bridge during the Blitz of WW2.

1943 I was evacuated with other children by train to Exeter in the west of England together with other London children to avoid the relentless bombing. I loved Devon so much that I never wanted to return home to the slums of London.

1947 I was collected from my happy home at Barton Place, Exeter by my father and taken home to the ruins of London. I was totally miserable there and ran away from 'home' several times to find my 'true' home in Exeter, much to the dismay of my parents whenever the police found me.

1951-55 I attended St Michaels' Catholic School, Keetons Road, Bermondsey and left school at age fifteen with no qualifications and no prospects of learning a trade - the school had been left badly damaged from the bombing and over thirty children had been killed while I was in Exeter; All exams were suspended until further notice.

1955-56 On leaving school at age fifteen I worked at many dead end, unskilled jobs, including a very small amount of time (two hours) under the railway arches near London Bridge, bottling imported rum. I was sacked on my first day for drinking the rum I was supposed to be bottling and becoming hopelessly drunk! Following many more labouring jobs, and long after leaving school, I decided to educate myself privately taking GCE's in English and German as well as gaining a degree in supervisory studies while serving with Hampshire Police, but before then I had applied to join the Merchant Navy and was accepted for training as a deck hand.

1956-59 I attended the Merchant Navy training school, 'Vindicatrix' at Sharpness near Bristol and learned all aspects of seamanship; sailing on nineteen different ships to many parts of the world, first as a lowly deck boy and then through the deck ranks until I was a fully fledged Able Seaman – visiting: Africa, America, New Zealand and a thousand miles up the Amazon River to Manaus picking up exotic timbers and running aground on mudbanks. We played football with the local Indians in a jungle clearing by the river surrounded by Piranha fish. The sea was a great adventure.

1960 Restless once more for new experiences Bill Haley arrived in England causing riots all over the country. This was followed by Jerry Lee Lewis. Music was now my first love and when home from the sea I made a beeline for the rock 'n' roll cellar clubs in Soho, London where British rock first started and it wasn't long before I was up on stage with the bands and musicians, strumming and singing alongside them

352

with my cheap Spanish guitar. It was there in Soho that I first saw Tony Sheridan sing and play and was immediately smitten by him. I was also lucky to be there when a German club owner arrived in Soho looking for an English rock band to play at one of his clubs in Hamburg and I never went back to sea again.

1960 The band included the greatly talented Tony Sheridan, and now I had the chance to play alongside him; In that first band, apart from Tony Sheridan, was Peter Wharton on bass guitar, Jimmy Ward on keyboard vocals and drums, Rick Hardy on vocals and guitar and myself on rhythm guitar and vocals too, We were a great success in Germany and I stayed there until I married Ingrid, my German girl friend. I intended to stay in Germany permanently, as Tony Sheridan had done but it didn't work out after I was sacked for threatening an abusive German co-worker with a shovel and then decided I would return to England. It was Johnny Watson the fabulous drummer and close friend who arranged somewhere for me to stay until I found work and a home in Southampton for Ingrid and our family and she joined me in the winter of 1963/64 .

1963 On arrival in Southampton I needed a job and somewhere to live. Finding work was easy and I started from the bottom again as a furniture salesman until I found something interesting and different as well as wanted to do

1965 Southampton Police were looking for new recruits and although I didn't hold out much hope I attended the interview, not expecting too much. But I got through and was accepted for training. Years later I asked the recruiting officer why he accepted me. He said I had 'been about a bit' in the Merchant Navy and was also as a musician;. The Police band needed some new members! He had little idea, bless him, that I only played rock music!

It wasn't long before I was transferred to the Criminal Investigation Department (CID) and became a detective. It was exciting as well as dangerous and I was commended several times both for bravery and for good detective work. I was promoted to Detective sergeant and again commended for tracking down a murderer together with a colleague. I was again promoted, the time to uniform Inspector and once again was commended for disarming a criminal in a siege situation.

1990-2015 After twenty five years with the Police Service I retired early to follow a new interest   in woodcarving, entering a hand-carved Celtic design chestnut wood   fireplace at the in the National Woodworker Show in London and was pleased to win the gold medal,

2015 My passion is now fixed on writing and I have now completed four manuscripts currently being made ready for publication, the first being, and the one you have just read: "Tony Sheridan, The One The Beatles Called The Teacher".

Colin Crawley

Other books coming soon by the same author:

"Tales of a Young Merchant Mariner"
A true sea-story of life at age sixteen in the British Merchant Navy.

"In search of Jim Corbett"
Based on a true story set in England and India when two boys one English one Anglo-Indian attempt to travel to India and join their hero Jim Corbett in the jungles of India.

"Journeys with Neon"
An strange space exploration story when a young human, Michael, is befriended by an alien explorer who invites Michael to join him on his exploration of other planets where shocking things happen to him.

24795363R00199

Made in the USA
San Bernardino, CA
06 October 2015